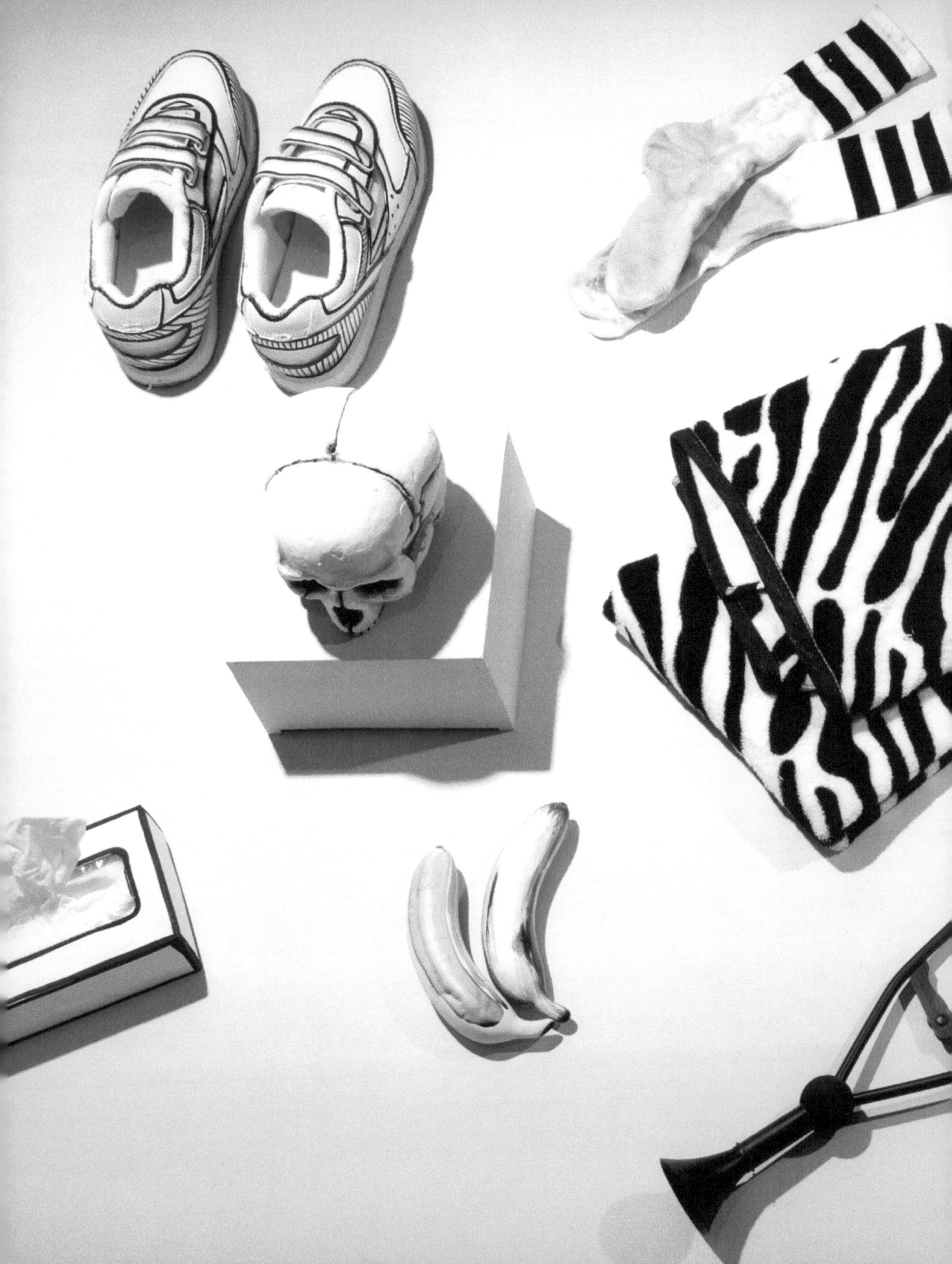

MARY
REID KELLEY

Working Objects and Videos

SAMUEL DORSKY MUSEUM OF ART
STATE UNIVERSITY OF NEW YORK AT NEW PALTZ

UNIVERSITY ART MUSEUM
UNIVERSITY AT ALBANY, STATE UNIVERSITY OF NEW YORK

CONTENTS

INTRODUCTION

We are delighted to present *Mary Reid Kelley: Working Objects and Videos*, an exhibition that brings together a rich trove of objects, paintings, drawings, and costumes along with the videos they inhabit. Through a combination of live action and animation, a barrage of puns and wordplay, and a fusillade of visual and literary references, Mary Reid Kelley examines historical eras of societal upheaval. Her characters grapple with change on a seismic scale, addressing us directly from behind their masks, painted faces, and bug eyes. They share the most intimate details of their lives: their fears, their missteps, and their determination to control their destinies—or, at the very least, sway them just a bit.

This is the first collaboration between the University Art Museum and the Samuel Dorsky Museum of Art, both part of the State University of New York system. We are grateful for the support and encouragement of our institutions, which make it possible for us to produce high quality exhibitions and publications. At the University at Albany, thanks to President Robert J. Jones, Provost and Vice President for Academic Affairs Susan D. Phillips, and Senior Vice Provost and Associate Vice President for Academic Affairs William B. Hedberg; at the State University of New York at New Paltz, thanks to President Donald Christian, Provost Philip Mauceri, and Interim Dean Paul Kassel.

Jessica Fredericks, Andrew Freiser, and the staff of Fredericks & Freiser Gallery have been helpful and supportive throughout the complex process of organizing the exhibition and catalogue. We are grateful for the generous loan of critical works from Leslie Cecil and Creighton Michael, Jennifer Danner, Robert Hobbs and Jean Crutchfield, the Hort Family Collection, and one anonymous lender.

The staffs of both museums worked diligently to make this project a success. At the Dorsky Museum, thanks to Curator of Exhibitions and Programs Daniel Belasco, Curatorial Intern Rachel Beaudoin, Program Manager Janis Benincasa, Graduate Assistant Steven Gordon Holman, Collections Manager/Registrar Wayne Lempka, Visitor Services Coordinator Amy Pickering, and Preparator Bob Wagner, as well as the many SUNY New Paltz faculty and staff who assisted with the media aspects of this project. At the University Art Museum, thanks to Registrar Darcie Abbatiello, Milton and Sally Avery Arts Foundation Intern Nicole Herwig, Exhibition Designer Zheng Hu, Exhibition and Outreach Coordinator Naomi Lewis,

Administrative Assistant Joanne Lue, Collections Production Coordinator Ryan Parr, Associate Director/Curator Corinna Ripps Schaming, and Preparator Jeffrey Wright-Sedam.

Both institutions owe a debt of gratitude to the foundations, corporations, and individuals that support our programs and help us realize our goals. For this exhibition, the Dorsky Museum is grateful to the Office of the President, the Office of the Provost, the School of Fine & Performing Arts, and the SUNY New Paltz Foundation. And from the University Art Museum, thanks to the Office of the President, the Office of the Provost, The University at Albany Foundation, and the Ellsworth Kelly Foundation.

Curator Daniel Belasco has done a masterful job organizing an exhibition that provides a fuller understanding of the flamboyantly artificial world of Mary Reid Kelley's videos; his essay presents the "working objects" in a context that allows for a deeper reading of the work. Corinna Ripps Schaming's interview with Mary Reid Kelley and Patrick Kelley sheds new light on their working methods and unique collaborative practice. Zheng Hu's elegant catalogue design has captured the sense and significance of the objects and the curatorial construct that gives form to the exhibition. Our hope is that there will be much here that is new to readers.

We feel fortunate to have had the opportunity to work with Mary Reid Kelley and Patrick Kelley. They have been unfailingly generous with their time and talents to help us realize the exhibitions and catalogue. They graciously opened their home and their studio to us, and it is now our great privilege to share that experience with others.

Sara Pasti
The Neil C. Trager Director
Samuel Dorsky Museum of Art
State University of New York at New Paltz

Janet Riker
Director
University Art Museum
University at Albany, State University of New York

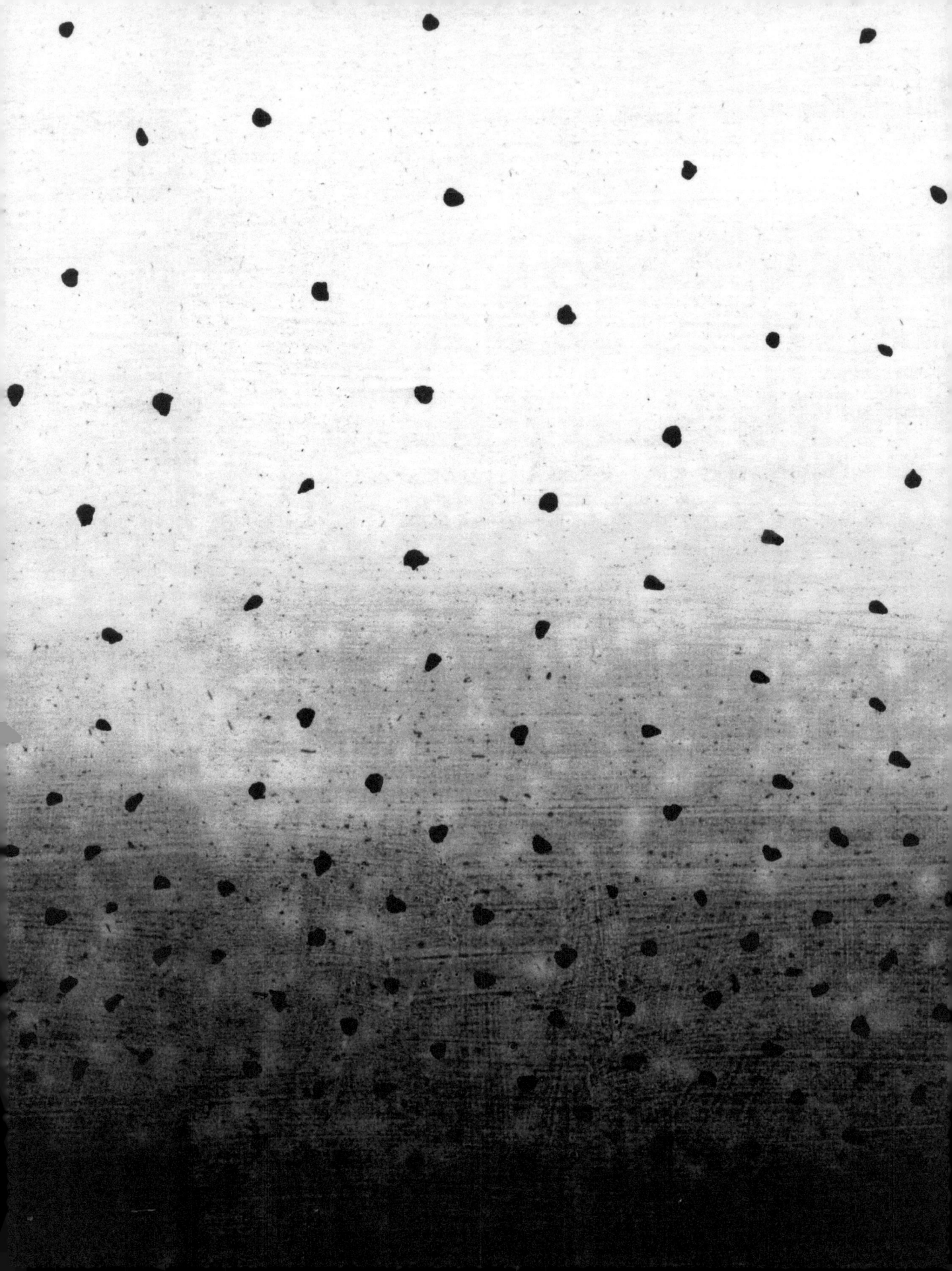

unreality effect

THE WORKING OBJECTS OF MARY REID KELLEY

By Daniel Belasco

Mary Reid Kelley (b. 1979) works in the vanguard of a generation that blends the digital and the analog to discourse with the millennia. From 2008 to the present, her astonishing videos have fused live performance, animation, drawing, sculpture, and digital design. Her poignant characters—a nurse, a prostitute, a bohemian, the Minotaur—confront the limits of their historical situations in droll verse. Blending Homer and Cindy Sherman by way of Virginia Woolf, Reid Kelley tells finely wrought narrative epics, rife with wordplay and art historical references, set in World War I, nineteenth-century Paris, and classical antiquity. Working with archival sources and a range of collaborators, especially Patrick Kelley, her husband and an accomplished artist, Reid Kelley invents a poetic mongrel media. By creating or manipulating all aspects of language, performance, and mise-en-scène, she rethinks the potential of the inauthentic to heighten our awareness of the real. The various drawings, hats, costumes, jewelry, and other items she uses reveal her comfort with mixing the hyper-real and the fake, the cheap and the lofty, to her own aesthetic ends. Barthes wrote of "the reality effect" as the presence of jarring factual detail in the fictional world of Flaubert.[1] Call Reid Kelley's practice the "unreality effect," where intensified artificiality excavates the mythic dimensions of individual integrity and political violence.

To date, Reid Kelley has produced six videos, or films, as she calls them. She created the first three—*Camel Toe* (2008), *The Queen's English* (2008), and

Texture (wallpaper),
2011

7

Sadie, The Saddest Sadist (2009)—as a master's student at Yale University School of Art. Shot in digital video with the aspect ratio of 4:3, the three can best be described as character studies of World War I actors at risk of emotional or physical disintegration: a combat pilot, nurse, and munitions factory worker, respectively. The fate of each is expressed and imagined through her or his amorous desires and sexual relations during wartime. The videos introduce Reid Kelley's main themes of self-delusion and hubris, which affect men and women, heroes and subalterns.

The second phase of Reid Kelley's video work began with *You Make Me Iliad* (2010), her first video shot in full HD with a 16:9 aspect ratio. *Iliad* continues to explore the poetic and sexual economies of World War I. As in *Sadie*, Reid Kelley performs the roles of both military man and fallen woman, but *Iliad* marks the expansion of her practice to include the production of a wide range of drawings, costumes, and props. Others perform for the first time, including her sisters Alice and Juliet and brother-in-law Micah. The theme of self-delusion becomes increasingly fragmented and conditional with the proliferation of characters, drawings, and objects here and in her two most recent videos, *The Syphilis of Sisyphus* (2011) and *Priapus Agonistes* (2013). These videos are more episodic and discursive, full of tangents and vignettes that do not advance a historically determined narrative but rather immerse the viewer in freeform visual and linguistic play.

Reid Kelley takes a painterly and graphical approach to melding a diverse array of two- and three-dimensional media into a cohesive black-and-white palette and flattened space. Like many video artists, she began her career as a painter, migrating to video to take advantage of the medium's expansive armature for aesthetic and historical inquiry. However, the transformative power of painting and drawing distinguishes Reid Kelley's videos from similarly capacious multimedia and performance-based videos by Paul McCarthy or Ryan Trecartin. After her videos are finished, Reid Kelley reconsiders them as sources for "character drawings" or portraits of the fully realized personages, such as the soldier in *Iliad* [pl. 1], sometimes set in backgrounds, as seen in *Sisyphus* [pl. 4]. The drawings are the culmination of her lengthy process, from research to writing to costume and prop design to performance to digital sets to editing. "They close the conceptual loop," she says of the character drawings.[2] The video's status as source for the character drawings inspires the interpretation of all of Reid Kelley's creative output as components of a larger whole. An exhibition of the full range of "working objects" (costumes, adornments, props, drawings, and furniture) she has created and adapted for her videos asserts their status as *gesamtkunstwerk*, or total work of art; every object, from a drawing to a glass bottle, bears her hand. Installed in three dimensions, these elements produce the larger-than-life space of opera or architecture, an experience that engages the senses and fully immerses us in an artist's unique vision.[3]

DRAWING AND PAINTING OF OBJECTS

Painting and drawing optically and materially knit together the objects, bodies, and scenery of Reid Kelley's videos, like graphical camouflage. The palette is black, white, and gray, evoking earlier ages of photography and television. The physical world of her videos, through the flattening effect of the monocular lens of the camera and the illusionistic effects of painting, reads like an animated painting. Reid Kelley takes the same illustrational approach toward the ready-made prop as she does toward sculpted, sewn, or drawn objects. A simple slash of white paint brings a black brush or a wine bottle into her visual universe. Ordinary shoes, hats, and garments are altered with a black or white border, outline, or highlight; contrasting black lines and geometrical shapes painted on the performers' white-painted skin transform the volumetric human form into a linear cartoon image. She also uses drawings and paintings on paper as visual elements of the videos. They function in three main ways: as backgrounds and scenery, as signs and components, and as textures and patterns.

Drawing as background scenery first appears in *The Queen's English*. Small drawings are scaled up in the digital sets. Two drawings, in one-point perspective and co-extensive with the video frame, depict the exterior and interior of a field hospital tent [fig. 1]. In *Sadie* and *Iliad*, a larger number of drawings create the four or five interior and exterior scenes. In *Sisyphus*, Reid Kelley produced significantly more drawings of interiors and exteriors for nearly twenty scenes. Some are historically accurate, while others demonstrate the theatricality of the sketched background. The street scenes of Paris, styled after the period photos of Charles Marville and prints of Edmond Texier,[4] are simplified geometrical shapes forming windows, doors, balconies, and the ubiquitous signage for wine [pl. 5]. Many short skits performed by the *saltimbanques* about Marie Antoinette [pl. 22], Diderot, Napoleon, Robespierre, and Baron Haussmann [pl. 19], among others, appear in front of a single drawn background rendered as a curtain, as if dropped in a vaudeville show.[5] The most fantastical interjections in *Sisyphus* have abstract or organically patterned backdrops, such as the drawings for the three mushrooms [pl. 28] and Sisyphus's polyamorous wedding. Notably, there are few comparable background drawings in *Priapus*, with the

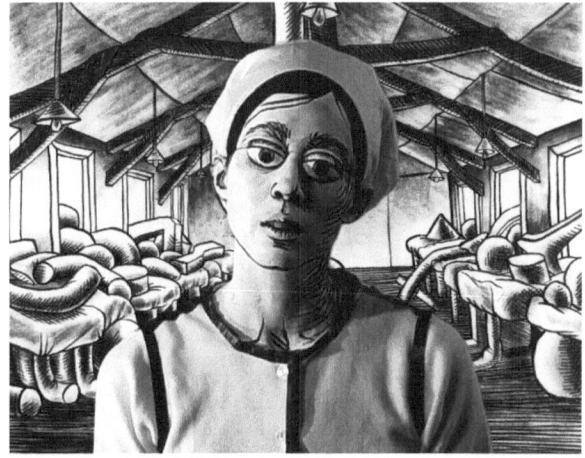

fig. 1
The Queen's English,
2008
Video still

exception of the Hades scene, which is an abstract suggestion of the void.

The second type of drawing—as two-dimensional sign or element—first appears in *Sadie*. Digital scans of these "component" drawings are inserted in the simulated three-dimensional sets designed and edited on computer. They function as intermediaries between the digital backgrounds and the analog props. In *Iliad*, the interior of the German soldier's bunker is a virtual portrait gallery [fig. 2], adorned with pictures of great German men of letters and politics like Goethe and Bismarck, all drawn by Reid Kelley with the same bug eyes that she uses to mask live performers [pl. 12]. A smaller group of three erotic drawings of women without bug eyes appears nearby [pl. 11]. These drawings represent the duality, in the soldier's worldview, of male as speaking subject and female as posing object. In *Sisyphus*, the protagonist's worldview is also expressed through aspirational portraits hanging in her garret [pl. 31], in this case "beauty heroes" modeled after Roman statues of empresses and goddesses [pl. 32]. Other component drawings in *Sisyphus* suffuse the urban landscape with posters, advertisements, and signs. Interior walls are also adorned with beauty ads, medical charts, and political messages. Many of these drawings are as small as 3 x 6 inches. In *Priapus*, most of the action takes place in the gymnasium, underground labyrinth, or Cretan landscape, overlooked by the craggy city of Knossos. Analog drawings of trees, bushes, and animals act as discrete visual elements in the digital landscape of rolling hills below a clear sky and puffy clouds [fig. 3]. For the gymnasium and labyrinth scenes, interior walls are a composite of material textures used as fill and drawn elements such as Minoan frescoes [fig. 4] and graffiti. With component drawings integrated into open-ended, amorphous digital scenery, the sense of space is more fluid in *Priapus*.

The third type of drawing, textures and materials, is created with oil stick, acrylic paint, or ink. Other textures (used in *Sisyphus*) include marble, wallpaper, and plaster. Considered as stand-alone works, they recapitulate moments of abstract painting, from the tactile monochromes of Robert Ryman to the op art of Bridget Riley. The most ambitious pattern was created for the cobblestone streets of Paris. Working in oil paint and referencing Leger's ovoid construction of

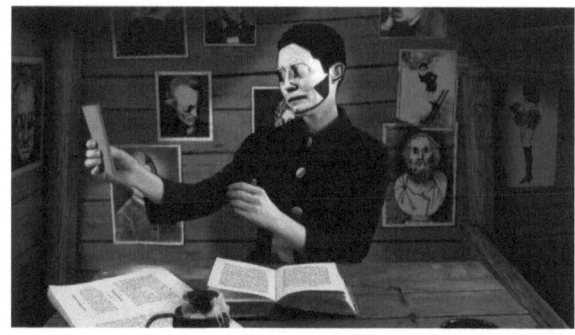

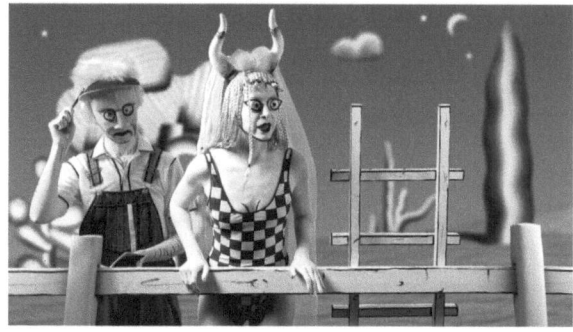

fig. 2
You Make Me Iliad,
2010
Video still

fig. 3
Priapus Agonistes,
2013
Video still

form, Reid Kelley rendered an intricate pattern on two sheets of paper [pl. 6]. The images at the edges of the long sides of the drawings match up, so they can be tiled in the digital set, giving the illusion on screen of endless cobblestones [fig. 5]. The same sort of abstract patterns—stripes, crosshatching, and shading—serve as textures on paper, objects, and costumes, such as the tall top hat worn by the dandy [pl. 8]. Some environments employ photographic sources found online. In *Iliad*, the walls, floors, ceilings, and other architectural elements of the bunker and the brothel have naturalistic textures from photographic images of wood grain, inspired by the look of expressionist films like *The Cabinet of Dr. Caligari* (1920). A photograph of bricks comprises the material imagery of labyrinth walls in *Priapus*.

    Type design and the visual impact of words is another realm where Reid Kelley employs drawing.

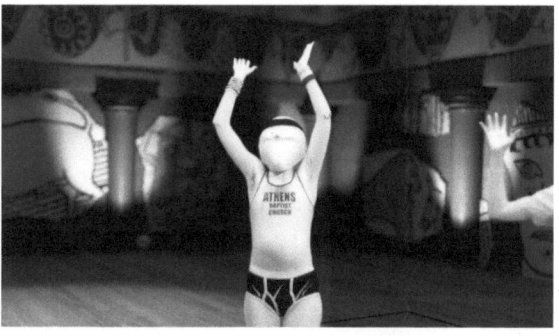

Many of her characters are seen writing or attempting to express themselves through poetry or correspondence. For *Sadie*, Reid Kelley made stop-motion animations of physical letterforms, choreographing letters from a vintage set of Mittens movie titlers so they are like a calligram in motion, a physical manifestation of punning and wordplay. In *Iliad*, three sets of laser-cut plastic type (Maximilian, Neuland, and Kabel) designed by German typographer Rudolf Koch, who fought in World War I, provide a more historically integrated visual design [fig. 6].[6]

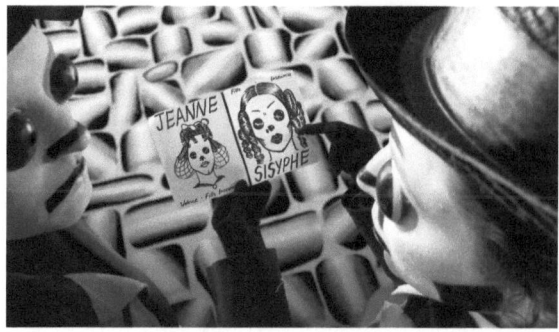

    As she shifts the temporal framework of her videos from the Great War, with its concern for mechanization, to earlier periods, Reid Kelley emphasizes the hand-drawn word. Drawn and painted signs dominate the

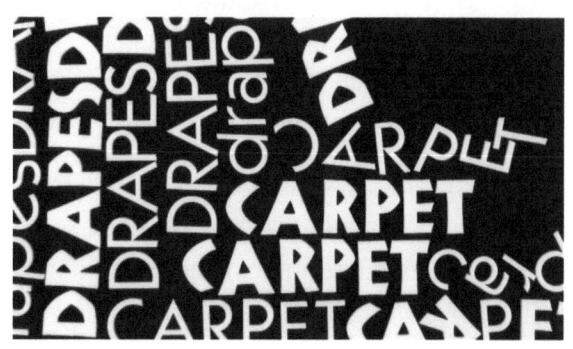

streetscape of mid-nineteenth-century *Sisyphus*. In *Priapus*, graffiti takes the place of commercial typography. The video's title, hand-inked in block letters, appears on the digital walls of the labyrinth, one of the thirty-three ink drawings used as graffiti [pl. 15]. The sexist words and caricatures allege the animal and sexual natures of the Minotaur and the Minoan women, chiefly Pasiphae and Ariadne [pl. 13], and recall the erotic graffiti on the brothel exterior in *Iliad*. The words visually represent the theme of insult and invective that runs through *Priapus*, inspired in part by the correlation of boasting in classical myth and contemporary hip-hop.[7]

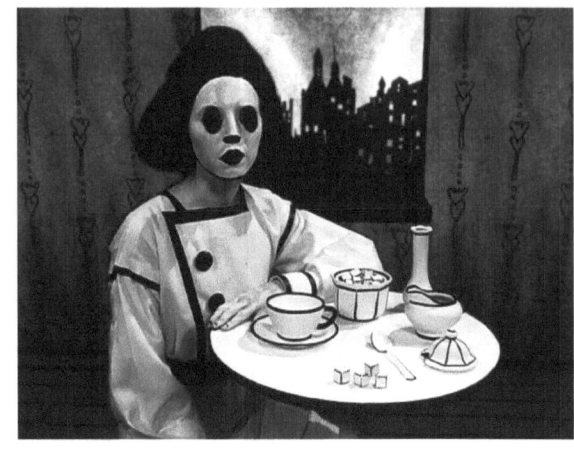

fig. 7
Sadie, The Saddest Sadist, 2009
Video still

OBJECTS, PROPS, AND FURNITURE

If drawings are infinitely scalable in the digital sets, the physical objects, props, and furniture are all actual size, relating directly to the human body. In the manner of a Dutch or Flemish portrait painter, Reid Kelley uses a discrete set of objects to define the social situation and fate of her characters. In *Sadie*, a teatime still life of cup and saucer, sugar bowl and spoon, sugar cubes, bud vase, and creamer sit before Sadie, seated at a café table [fig. 7]. Sadie handles the objects, thus placing her in a more three-dimensional space than that of the blank or flat backgrounds of *Camel Toe* and *The Queen's English*. Painted white with black outlines, the objects resemble the reductive imagery of a diagram. In *Iliad*, however, Reid Kelley does not blanket props in starkly artificial black-and-white paint. She alters them in some ways, such as adding a translucent layer of white acrylic paint or affixing handwritten labels, but she preserves the original color of the objects' materials: glass, metal, rubber, or wool. Objects are more artifacts than transformative elements in *Iliad*, despite their function in character development and the visualization of a few choice puns, such as the German Imperial army slogan *Gott Mit Uns*, meaning "God with Us," sewn on three wool mittens [fig. 8]. The naturalism of *Iliad* exposes the limitations of historicity in storytelling and deviates from Reid Kelley's normal practice of the "unreality effect," perhaps an expression of her frustration with not finding any archival documentation of the lives of Belgian prostitutes on the Western Front.

Sisyphus returns to the splendor of the synthetic, and more specifically thematizes the relationship between gender roles and objects. The character of Sisyphus is a satirical embodiment of Baudelaire's ideal modern woman who elevates fashion into spiritual art, as Baudelaire describes in the "In Praise of Make Up" section of his essay, *The Painter of Modern Life*.[8] As with *Sadie*, the video

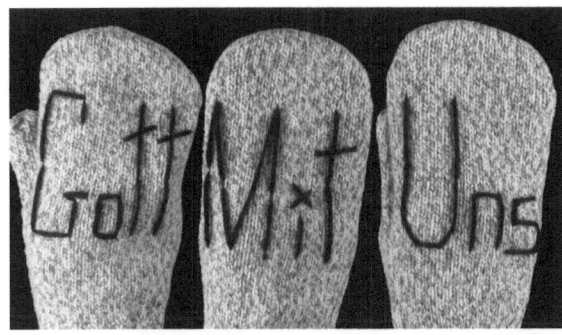

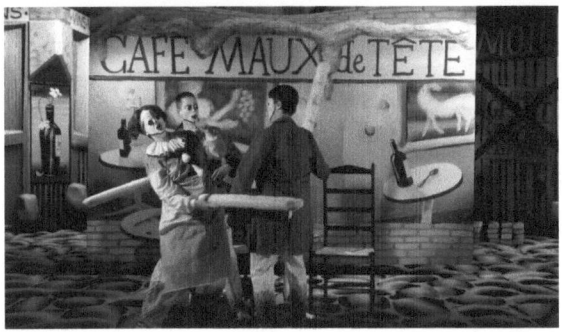

opens with the female protagonist sitting among personal effects. Here, Sisyphus appears before multiple black bottles, makeup pots, brushes, and flowers, all visually accented with white paint. The vanity also bears decayed fruit, recalling the *vanitas* themes of traditional still life painting and representing both Sisyphus's hatred of the limits of nature and her unavoidable fate as a woman to be considered part of nature. Containers of fluids symbolize the mutable societal situation of Sisyphus, like Sadie and the unnamed prostitute in *Iliad*. Objects convey gender stereotypes. Women can be seen holding objects related to appearances and self-absorption: mirrors for Sisyphus and Pasiphae, a tube of hand lotion for Venus, a spindle of thread for Ariadne. In contrast, the male authorities portrayed in *Sisyphus* and *Priapus* use instruments of measurement, observation, and construction: a globe for Diderot, a stethoscope and listening device for the asylum doctors, and a hammer for Daedalus. Assassin Charlotte Corday, appearing in *Sisyphus*, is the lone exception, using a painted wooden knife (also used by Jesus in the interjection scene set in the manger) to murder Marat.

To escape the dependence of narrative on gendered objects, Reid Kelley uses the interruptive energy of irony and the visual pun. Freeing words from fixed meanings, puns realize the potential for language to harbor anarchy and disassociate forms from habits. The prop as punch line, explored in limited ways in earlier videos, is expressed in full force in *Sisyphus*, perhaps as a release from the mounting crisis of Sisyphus's life as she is on the path to an asylum. The comedic devices of *commedia dell'arte* and slapstick run rampant. A number of the short vignettes culminate in props and objects that literalize puns. In a Marx

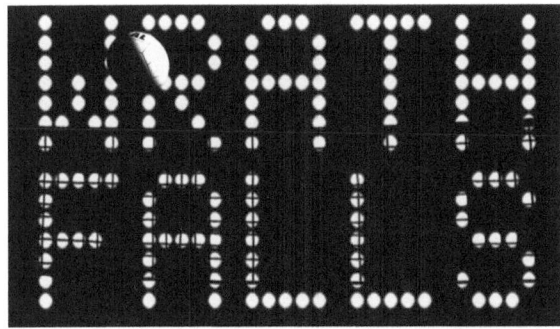

Brothers-inspired scene, family members jest "I beget you" while bashing each other with baguettes made from white spray-painted foam swimming noodles [fig. 9]. Sisyphus's pun on amoral/a morel gives way to the most surrealistic moment in Reid Kelley's oeuvre, the Lewis Carroll-esque silliness of three singing mushrooms played by human actors. The morel headpiece, made of chicken wire, papier-mâché, and spray foam, is an enlarged version of the exquisite model in polymer clay handled by Sisyphus [pl. 29].

Theatrical apparatus, such as fake snow shakers, indicate the shift in tone of Reid Kelley's videos from the World War I social critique of her first four works to history and myth as fodder for masquerade. After the sober naturalism of *Iliad* and the exuberant theatricality of *Sisyphus*, *Priapus* is an expanded version of the illustrational black-and-white aesthetic established in *Sadie*. Reid Kelley is especially economical with the props used in *Priapus*. The volleyball [pl. 24], Minotaur baby [pl. 16], and Pasiphae's oversized teacup and saucer and tissue box work to both advance the narrative and visualize puns.

MASKS, COSTUMES, AND ACCESSORIES
Costumes are subjected to the same formalized aesthetic as the props and scenery. Other than the green and gray uniforms adorned with polymer clay and acrylic gray buttons in *Iliad*, nearly every other costume in Reid Kelley's videos is white or black, with edges outlined in the contrasting color and drawn, painted, taped, or sewn. The costumes rarely call attention to themselves, merging with the overall look of the video's design. The rare patterned garment—Pasiphae's checkerboard swimsuit, Venus's polka-dotted bustier [fig. 11], Sisyphus's striped gown [pl. 3], and Charlotte Corday's geometric dress [pl. 18]—adds ornamental flourish and perhaps also indicates that a female character possesses a degree of nerve. Highly sexualized, the bodysuit costumes of *Priapus*—the abundant pubic hair of Pasiphae and the Minotaur [pl. 17] and the athletic supporter of Priapus [fig. 12]—parody the heroic nudes depicted in ancient sculpture, vases, and frescoes.

The egg-shaped forms that cover the eyes transform the performers into living cartoons who inhabit a space of imagination and illusion. Modeled from polymer clay and painted white, each pair is unique, with different treatment of the pupils; strips or loops of black fabric, or holes, make the character appear sad, intelligent, lusty, or deranged. The eye covers are one of Reid Kelley's signature moves as she works with the black-and-white palette and poetic language to define her individual style. Covering "the windows to the soul," the eyepieces effectively serve as masks, blocking the performers' identities and endowing new ones.

In *Priapus*, Reid Kelley first introduces total head masks, partly because she plays every character. Reid Kelley ordered the neoprene masks for the anonymous Greek chorus [pl. 26] and volleyball players from a theatrical supplier in Indiana, added details and other elements in polymer clay, then applied gesso and acrylic. The faces of the main characters are highly exaggerated. Venus is a pug; Priapus has a fish for an eye patch, secured by a headband [fig. 13]; Pasiphae wears a blonde cornrow wig [fig. 14] and sunglasses that cover her teardrop-shaped eyes. The Minotaur has a bull face and a paper bag headdress, which contains one of the many personal references in *Priapus*: the letters "Be Lo" can mean "below," where the labyrinth is, but also refer to the "BI LO" supermarket in the South Carolina of Reid Kelley's childhood. Church volleyball games are also a youthful memory. The masks assert Reid Kelley's shift from a historically based narrative to a mythic one laced with overt references to contemporary American culture.

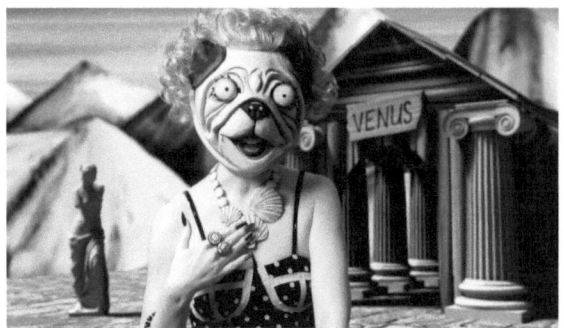

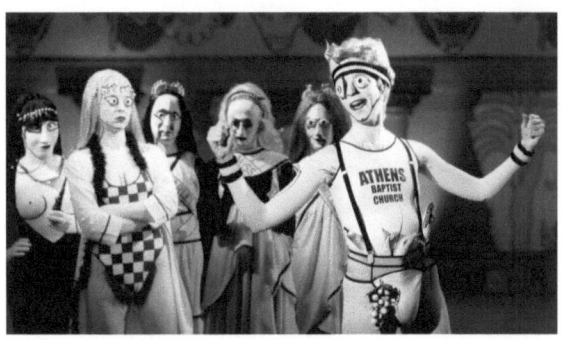

In addition to dress and attire, the personalities in Reid Kelley's videos are expressed through wearable pieces like hats, shoes, and jewelry. The soldiers of *Iliad* sport helmets and belts that distinguish their ranks and fealty to the Kaiser. Reid Kelley's intensive historical research informed details like the metal rivets randomly affixed to the soldier's helmet and the ornate spiked

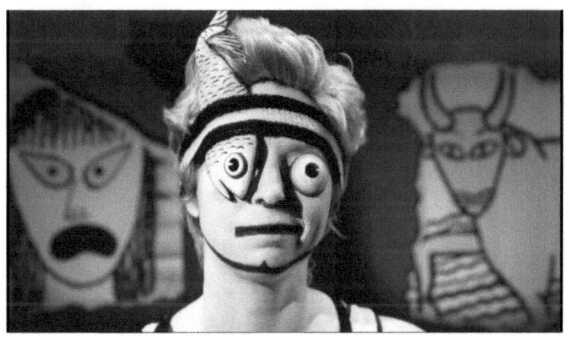

fig. 11, 12, 13
Priapus Agonistes, 2013
Video stills

pickelhaube of the medical officer [pl. 2]. The varied historical figures in *Sisyphus* wear top hats, bowlers (anachronistically, she admits), Phrygian hats, and wigs. While headwear is varied and important in its proximity to the speaker's face and mouth, feet and shoes are rarely visible. In *Iliad*, the only feet shown are those of the Belgian prostitute standing in the basin as she douches, emphasizing her naked powerlessness [fig. 15]. Most bodies are shown from the torso up, with a few exceptions. In *Sisyphus*, long shots of outdoor scenes display the full standing bodies of the *saltimbanques* [fig. 16], Charlotte Corday, and Sisyphus. In *Priapus*, we only see the full bodies of a character when she or he is prone, such as Pasiphae in grand odalisque.

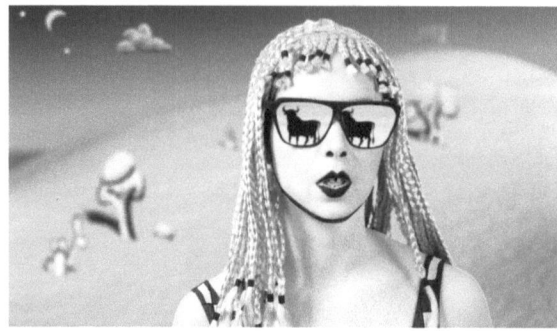

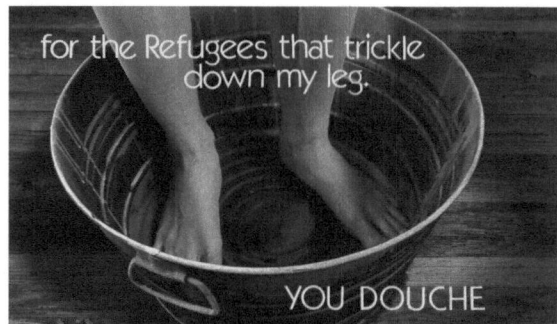

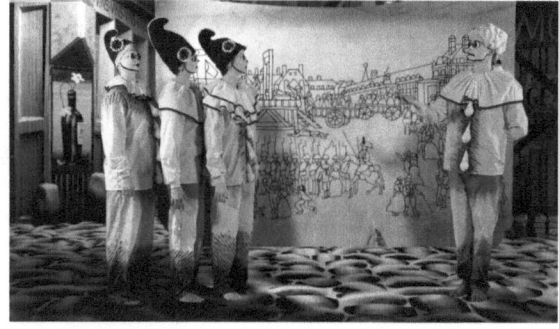

Costumes and masks are far more important in defining character in *Priapus* than are objects or props. Focusing on the movement and performance of the body, *Priapus* has no still life scenes equivalent to those in *Sadie*, *Iliad*, and *Sisyphus*. Instead, costume jewelry and personal adornments are used to define the characters. Crafted in polymer clay and painted in acrylic, they have a chunky elegance. Venus is the most ornamented, with four rings and two bracelets with geometrical designs and a necklace with scallop shells that evokes her marine origin. Her long black fingernails complete the decked-out look. Pasiphae sports only Wayfarer-style sunglasses, the epitome of cool, making her and Daedalus, with his overalls and visor, two anachronistically attired characters in *Priapus*. More classically attired in drapery, Ariadne wears a symbolic necklace, in this case a snake, a reference to her association with the Minoan snake goddess.

Priapus is the only male character in a Reid Kelley video to possess a cluster of non-uniform adornments that reveal his persona. A hypersexual symbol of fertility, often depicted in antiquity with an oversized phallus, he wears a belt loaded with a bunch of grapes, other fruits, and fish, symbolizing abundance and fecundity. The bananas and peppers are humorously unsubtle. He is the masculine version of the "eternal feminine," defined by sexuality and the body. Unlike the female characters who resent their entrapment in sexualized bodies, and the male characters who resent their dependence on women, Priapus is perhaps the

fig. 14
Priapus Agonistes,
2013
Video still

fig. 15
You Make Me Iliad,
2010
Video still

fig. 16
The Syphilis of Sisyphus, 2011
Video still

most self-satisfied character in a Reid Kelley video, though he may only be escaping with his delusions intact.

The consideration of Reid Kelley's working objects, costumes, and drawings offers a new approach to her videos. By organizing and categorizing the physical structures and expressive patterns of each video, we can better understand how Reid Kelley manipulates modes of history, language, gender, and period style. She has described the strict parameters of poetry, such as rhyme and meter, as a form of showy artificiality in language.[9] Verse is formalized and constructed language, not natural, but all the more beautiful and meaningful because of the craft revealed in the manipulations. Reid Kelley takes a similarly artificial and formalized approach to vision. The materiality of the working objects is central to Reid Kelley's use of the "unreality effect" to enhance the fake to reveal new truths.

[1] Roland Barthes, "The Reality Effect," trans. Richard Howard, in *The Rustle of Language* (New York: Hill and Wang, 1987), pp. 141-148.

[2] Mary Reid Kelley interview with author, September 20, 2013.

[3] The first installation of Reid Kelley's costumes and drawings alongside video was the exhibition of *The Syphilis of Sisyphus* at Fredericks & Freiser, New York, in fall 2011.

[4] Edmond Texier, "Tableau de Paris," Paulin et Le Chevalier, 1852.

[5] After completion of the video, Reid Kelley returned to some of these working drawings and repurposed them as elements of collages, which function as unique artworks.

[6] Reid Kelley is especially fascinated by the long life of the typeface Neuland and how it came to be associated with the exotic and savage, appearing on Harlem Renaissance anthologies and the logo for the blockbuster movie *Jurassic Park* (1993).

[7] For her comparison of hip-hop to classical myth, see Mary Reid Kelley, "500 Words," *ArtForum*, August 14, 2013, http://artforum.com/words/id=42417

[8] Charles Baudelaire, *The Painter of Modern Life and Other Essays* (London and New York: Phaidon Press, 1995)

[9] Tyler Green, "Mary Reid Kelley," *The Modern Art Notes Podcast*, July 25, 2013, http://manpodcast.com/search/Mary+Reid+Kelley.

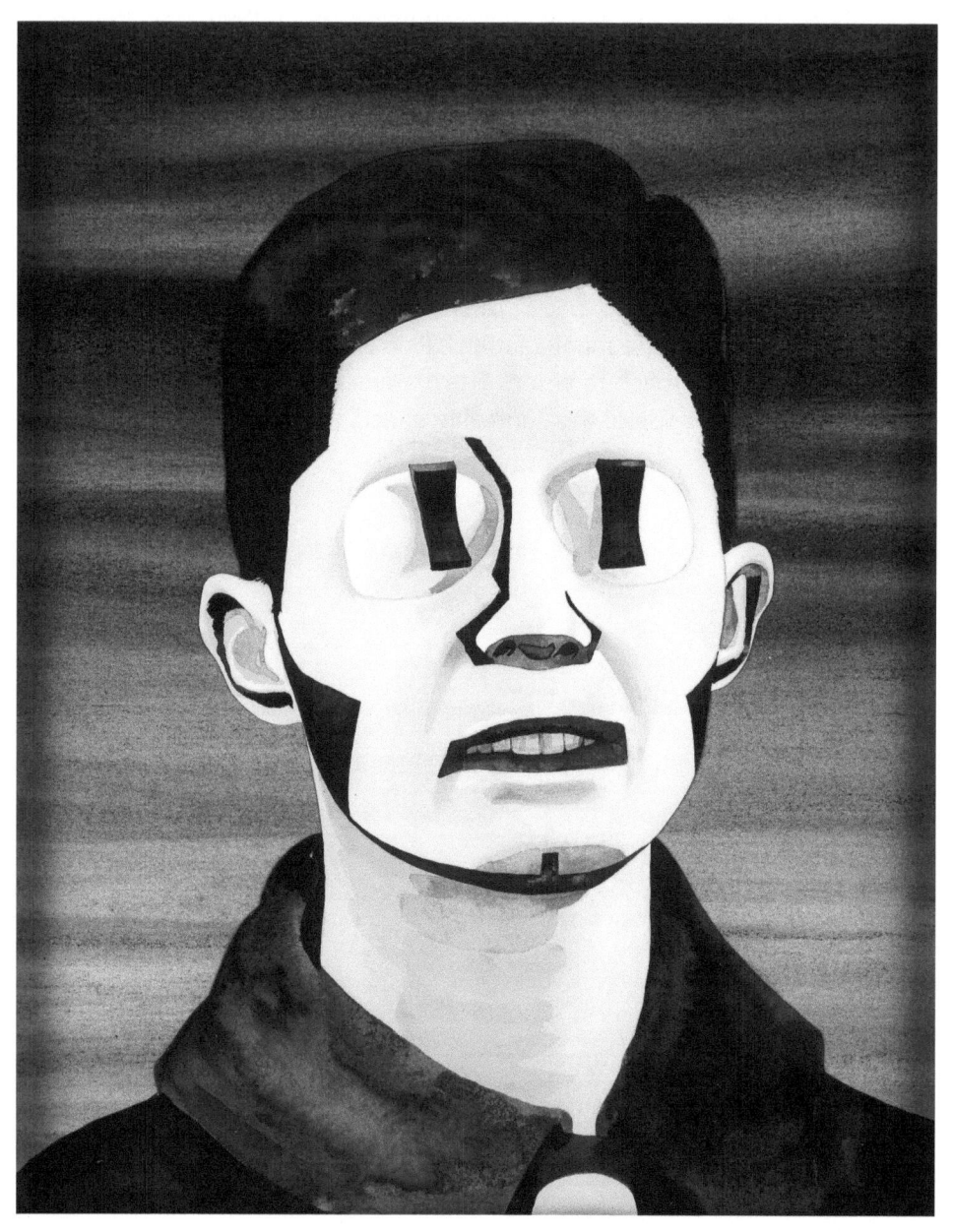

Pl. 1
Soldier, 2010
Ink, acrylic paint, and charcoal on paper

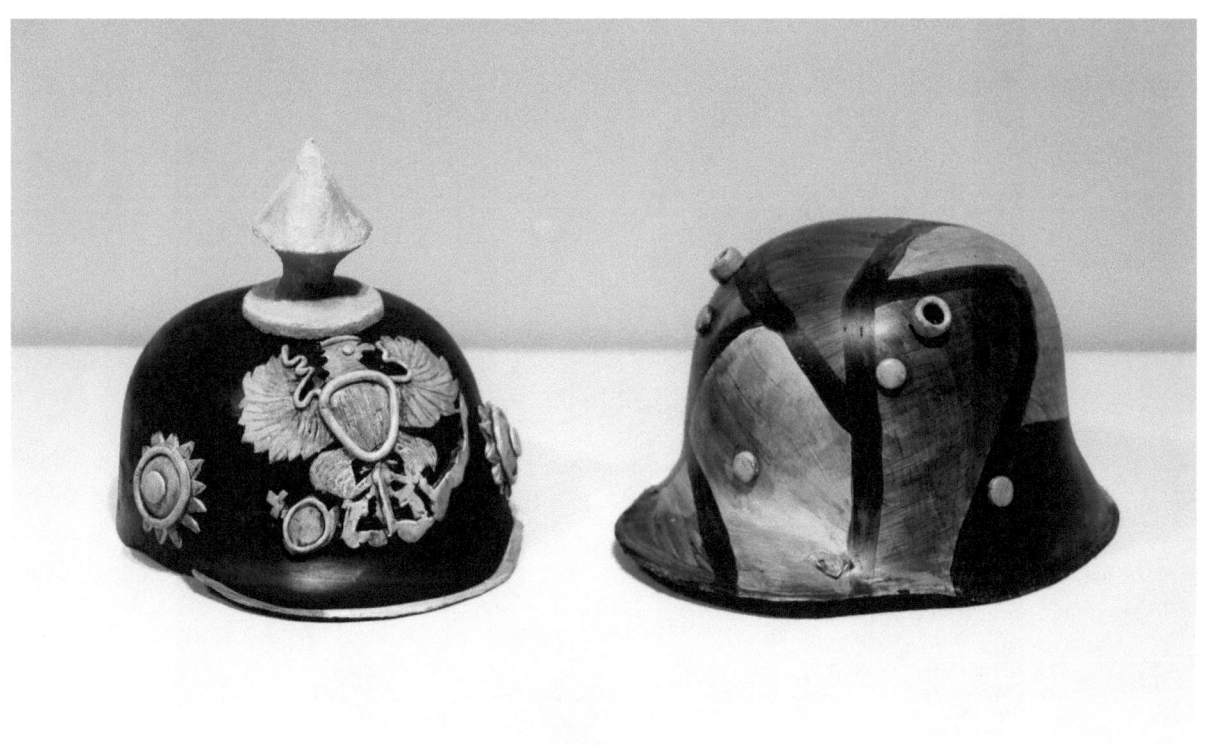

Pl. 2

LEFT: Medical Officer's Pickelhaube, 2010
Plastic, polymer clay, Styrofoam, and acrylic paint

RIGHT: Soldier's Helmet, 2010
Plastic, buttons, polymer clay, and acrylic paint

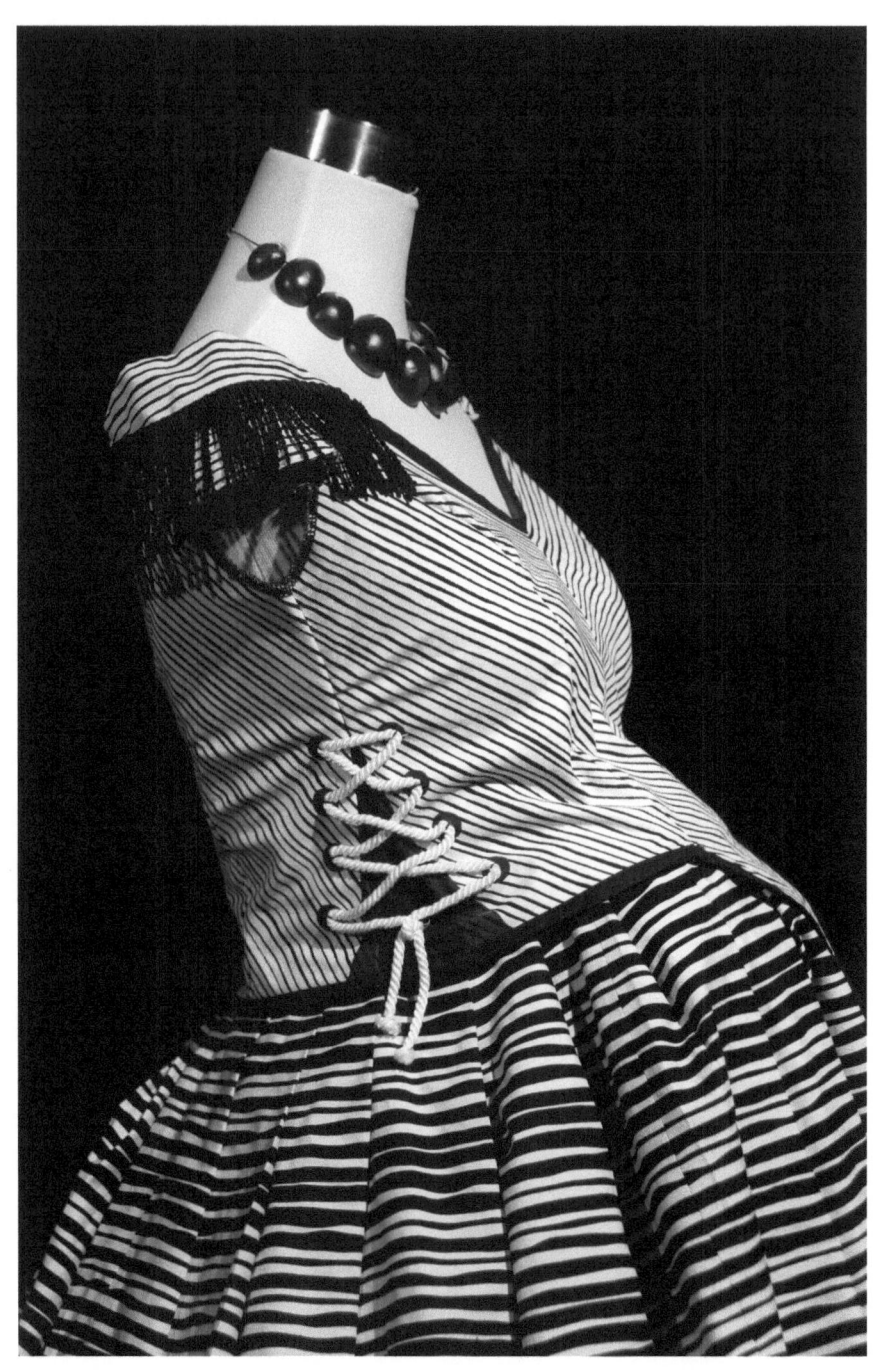

Pl. 3
Sisyphus's Gown, 2011
Cloth, ribbon, tassel, lace, foam, and hoop skirt;
Necklace: polymer clay and acrylic paint

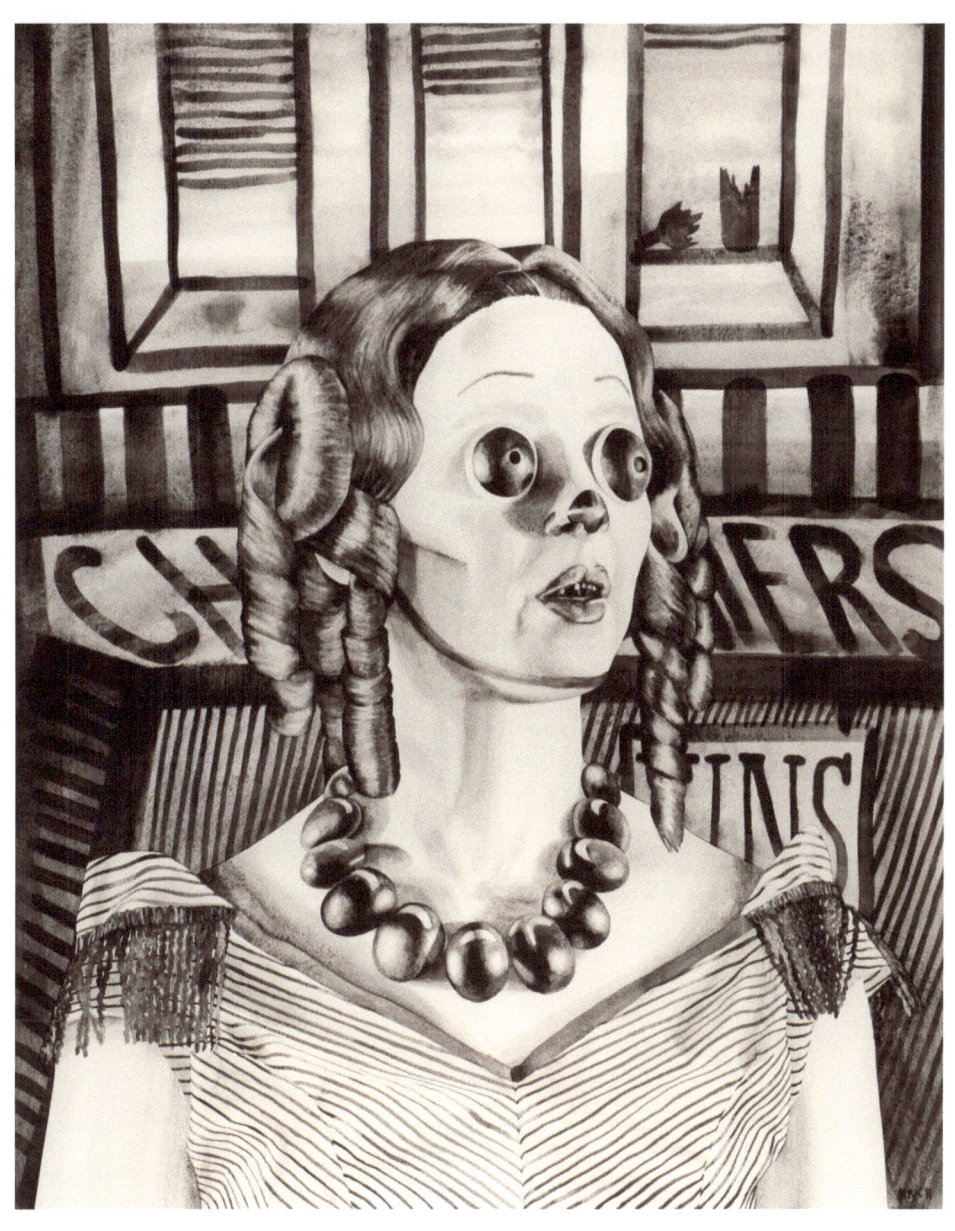

Pl. 4
Sisyphus (Chiffonniers' Vins), 2011
Collage and watercolor on paper

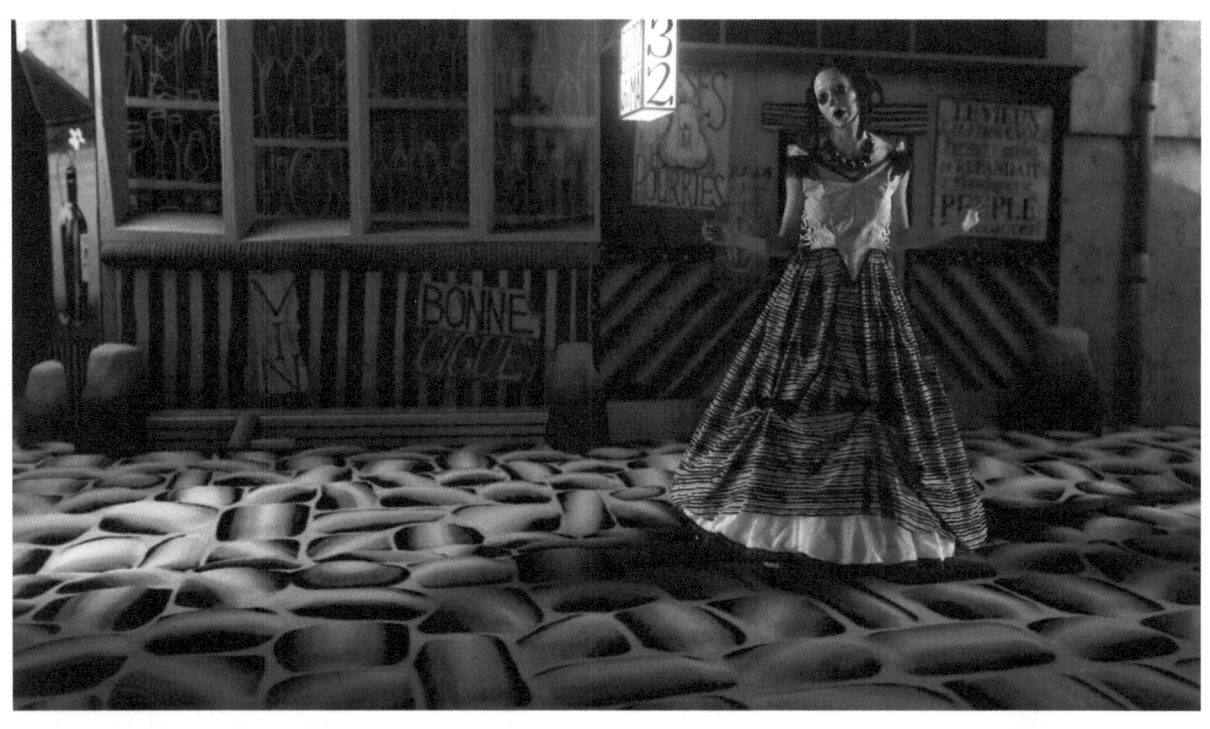

Pl. 5
The Syphilis of Sisyphus, 2011
Video still

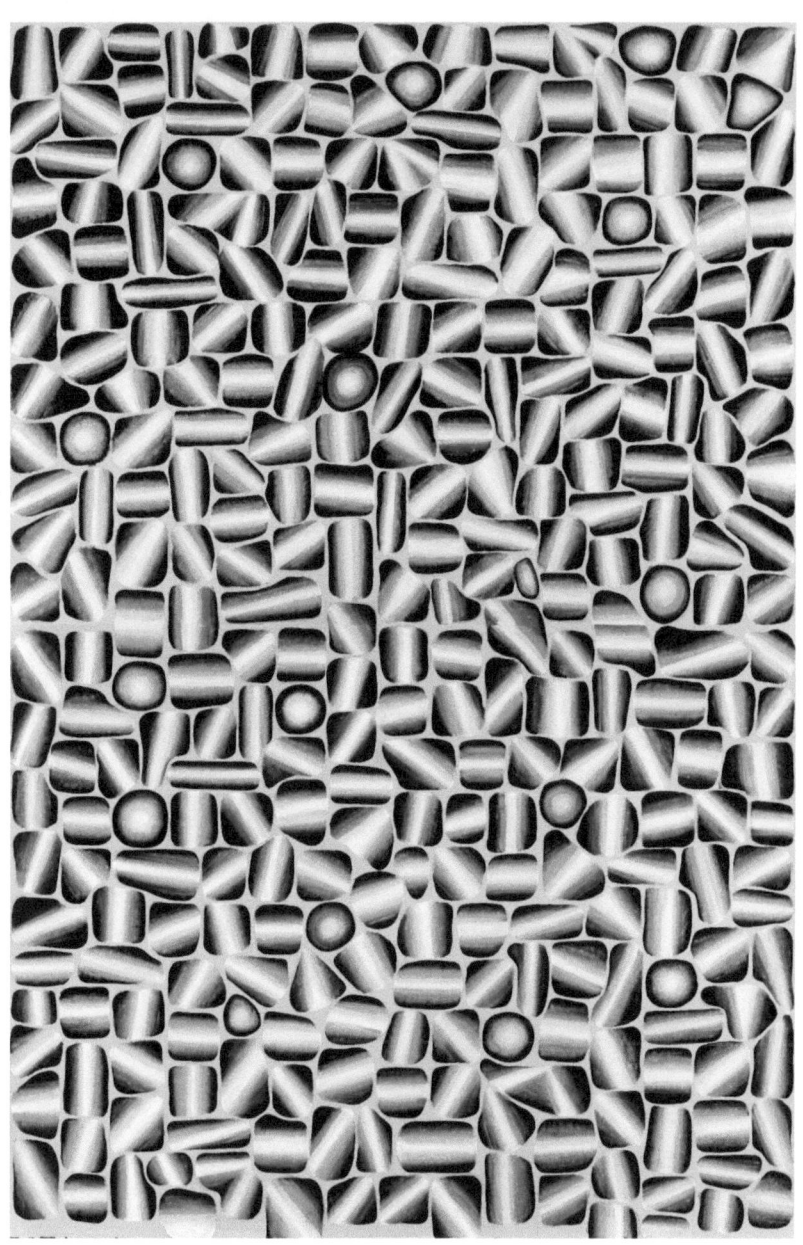

Pl. 6
Texture (Cobblestones), 2011
Oil and acrylic paint on Stonehenge
paper, two sheets

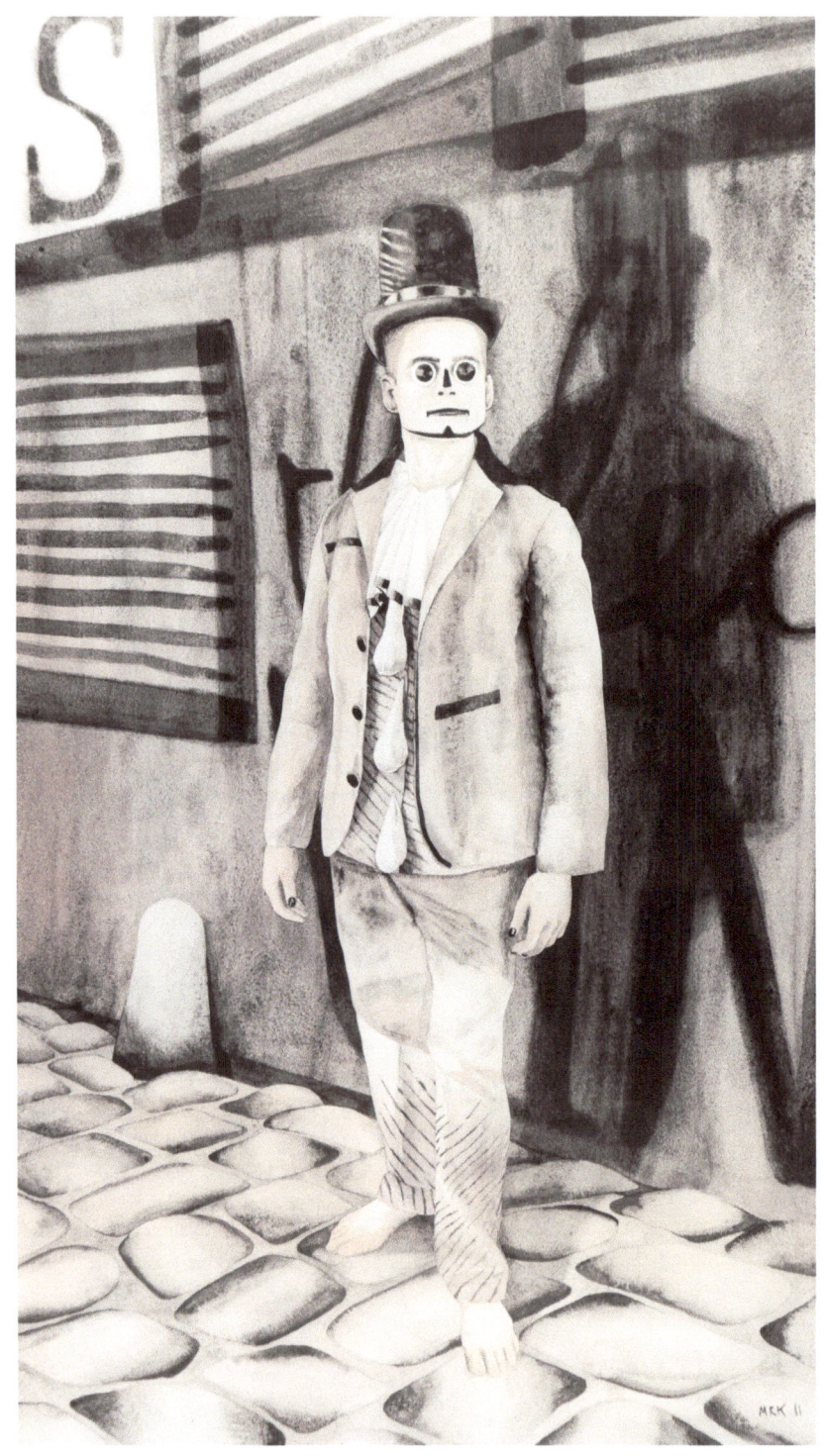

Pl. 7
Dandy Saltimbanque, 2011
Collage, watercolor, and acrylic
paint on paper

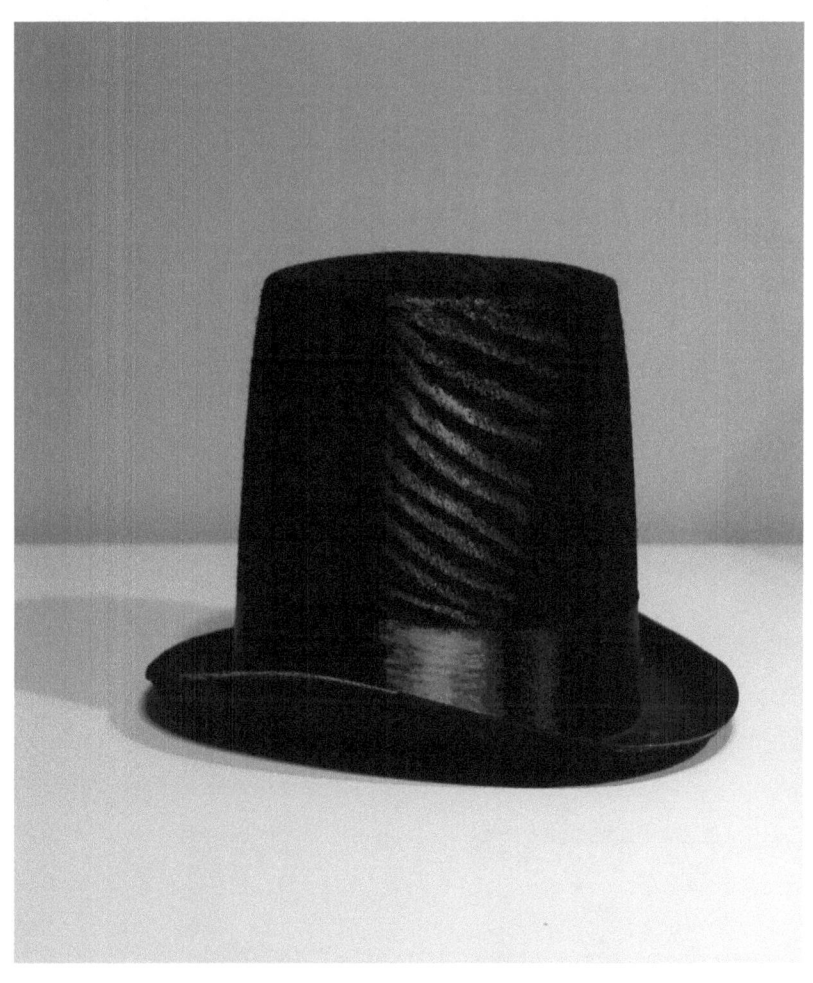

Pl. 8
Dandy's Top Hat, 2011
Felt, plastic, ribbon, and oil stick

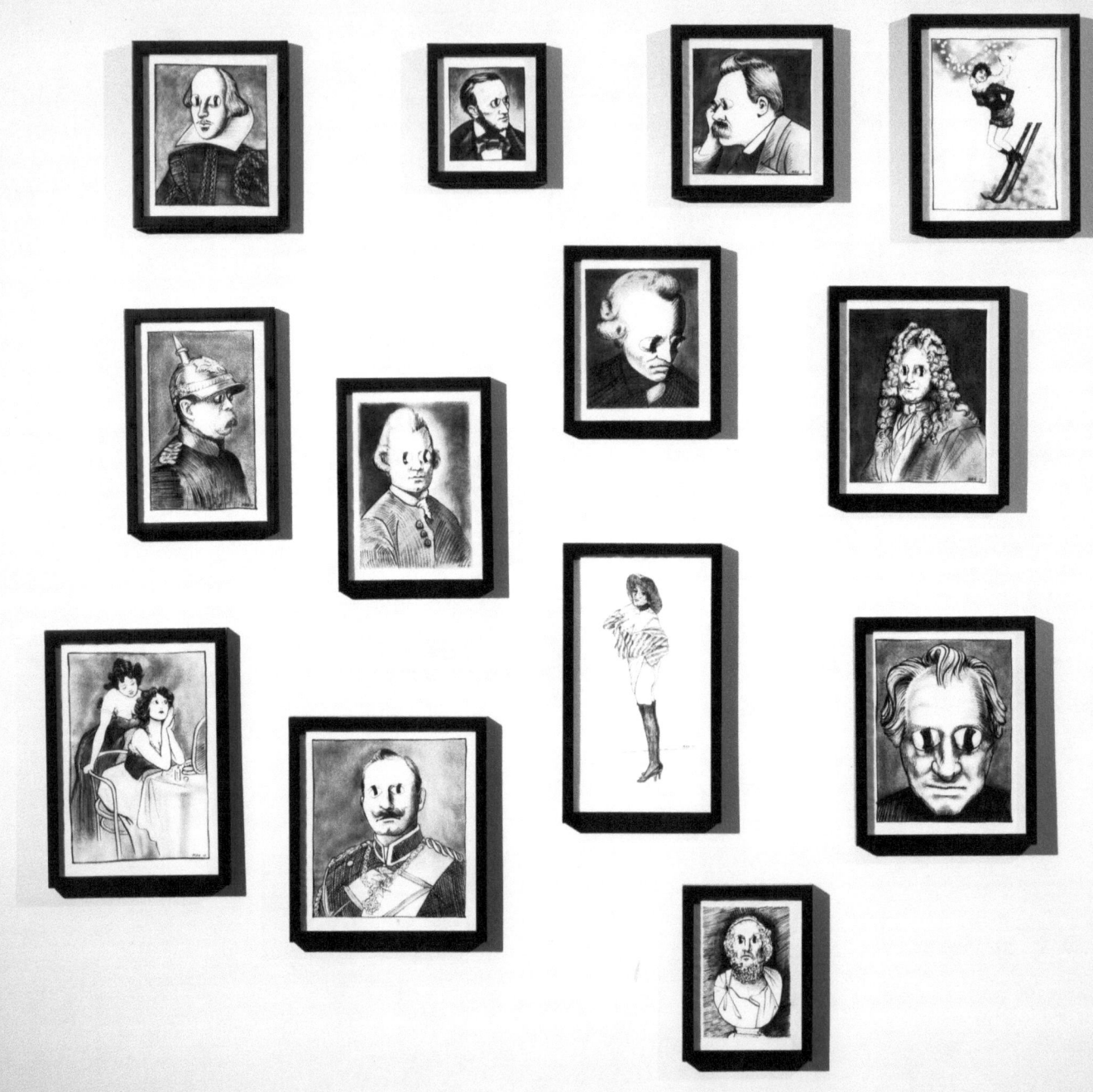

Pl. 9
Iliad Portraits, 2010
Installation view, Samuel Dorsky Museum of Art
Ink and graphite on vellum

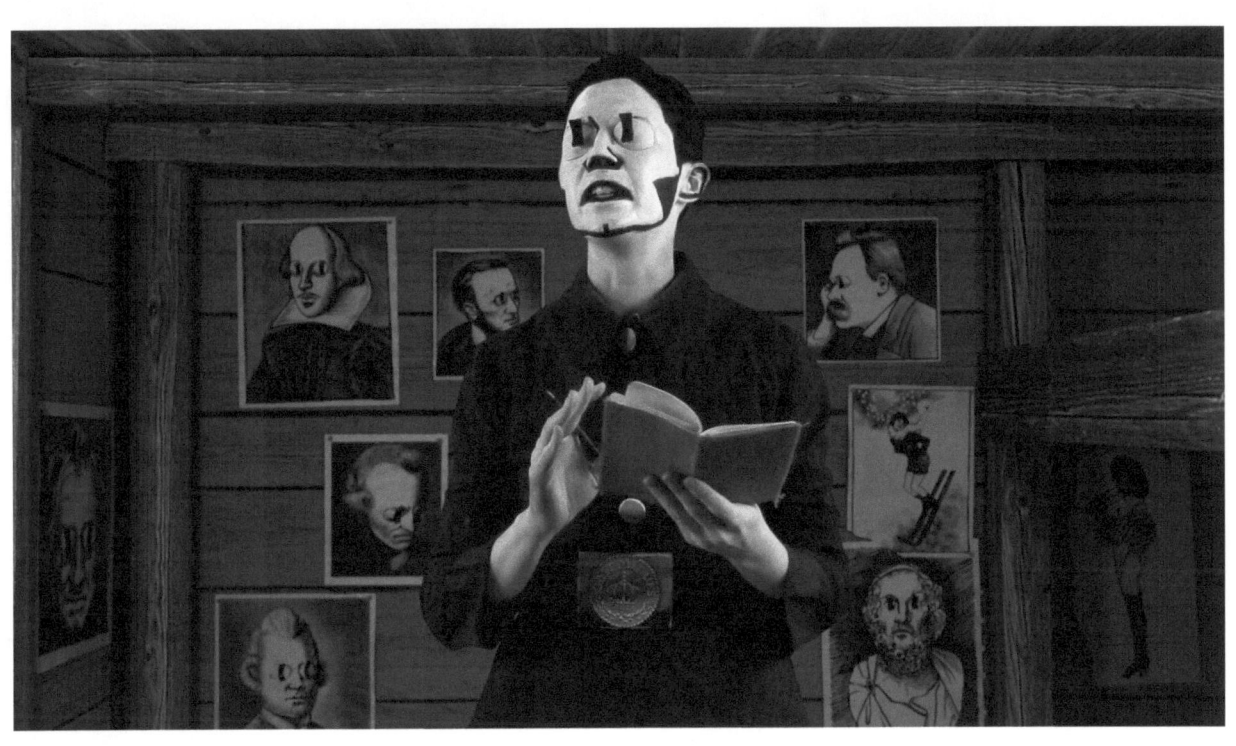

Pl. 10
You Make Me Iliad, 2010
Video still

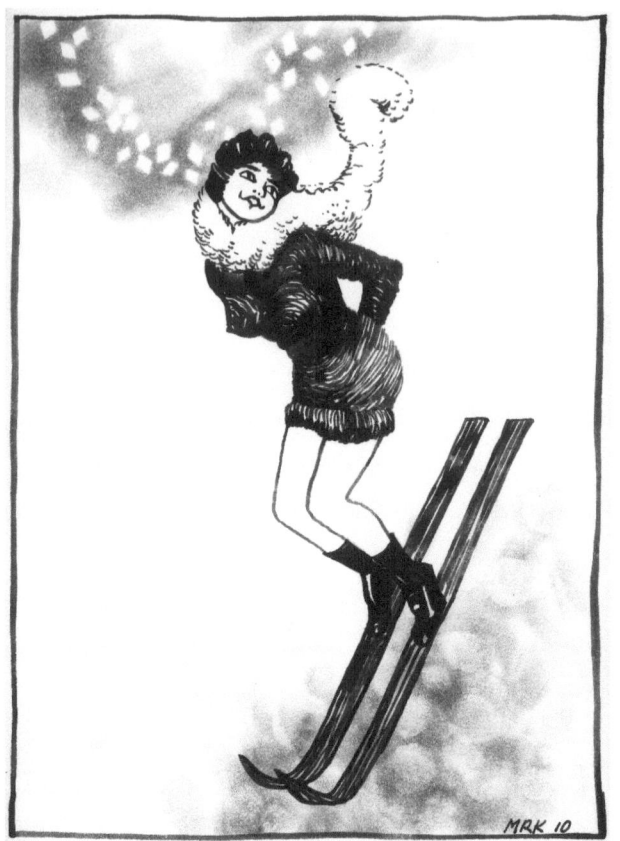

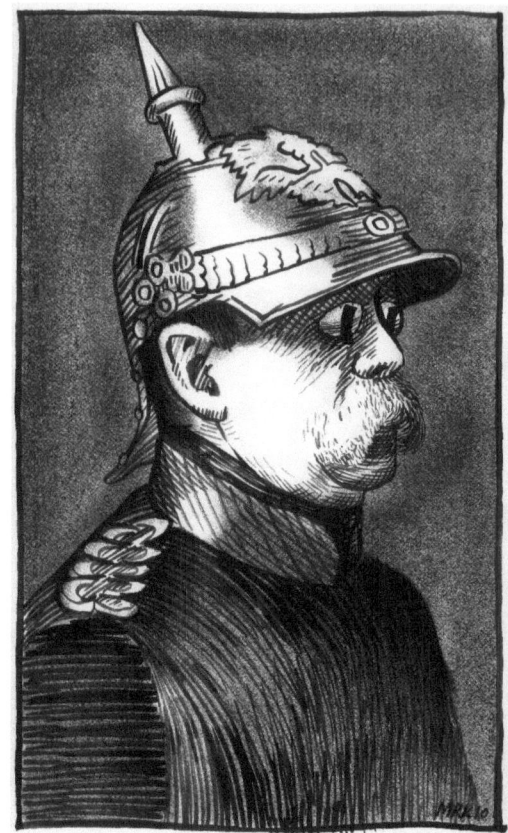

Pl. 11
Ski Girl, 2010
Ink and graphite on vellum

Pl. 12
Bismarck, 2010
Ink and graphite on vellum

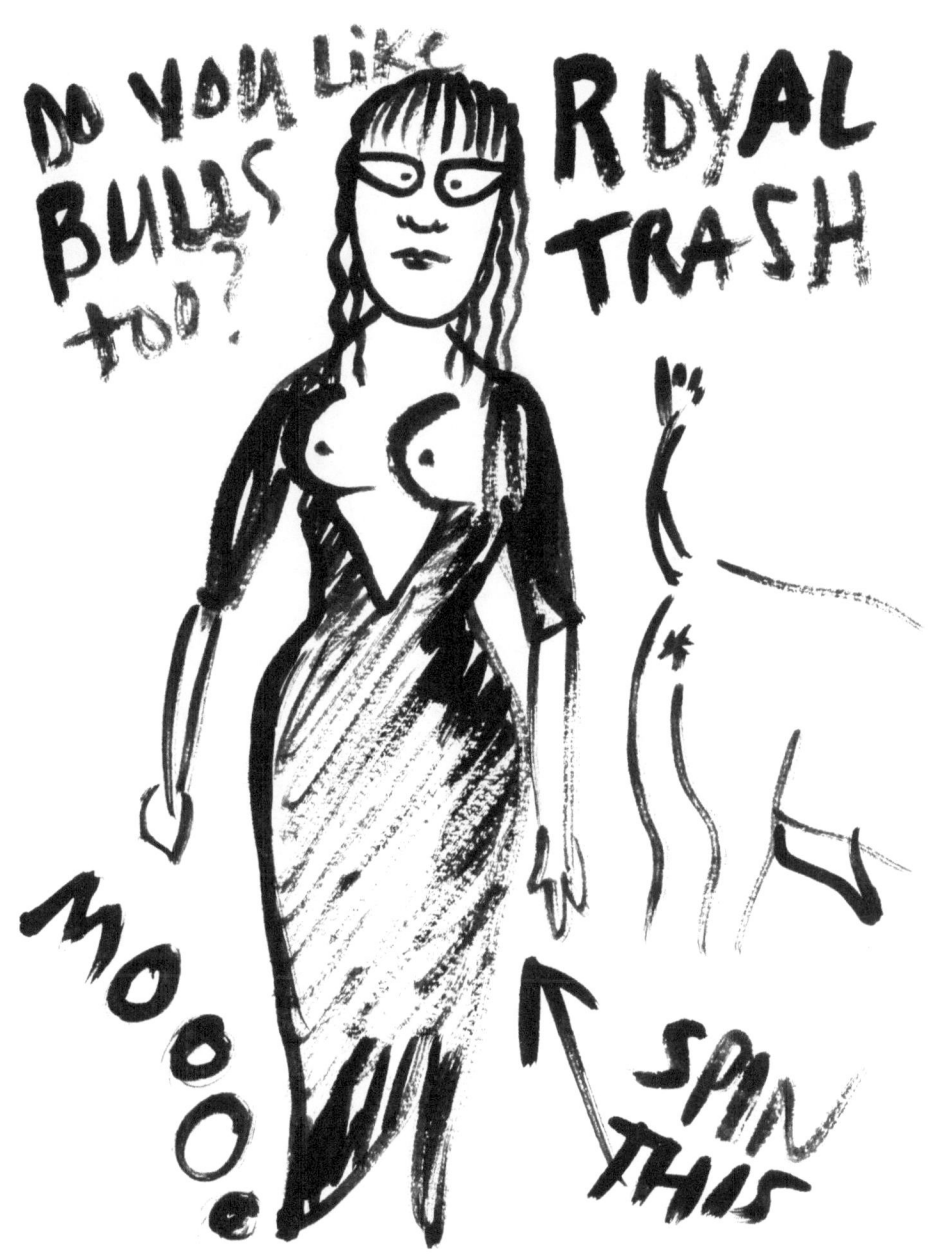

Pl. 13
Labyrinth Graffiti (Ariadne), 2013
Ink on paper

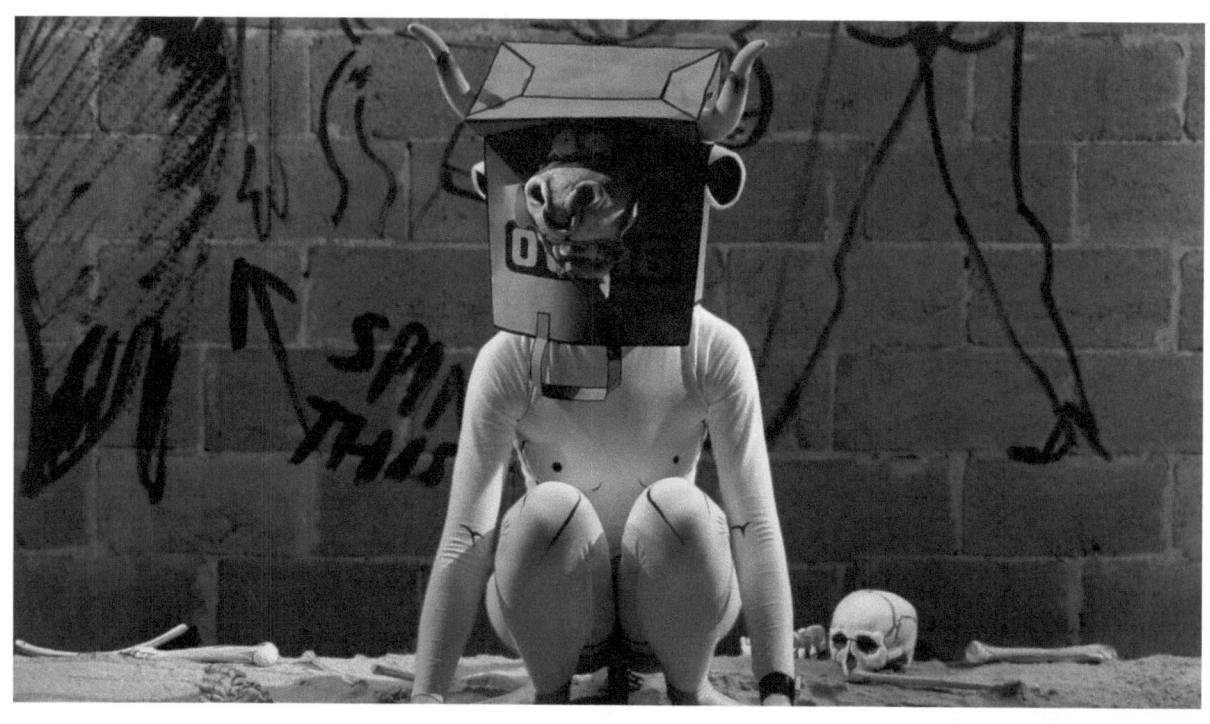

Pl. 14
Priapus Agonistes, 2013
Video still

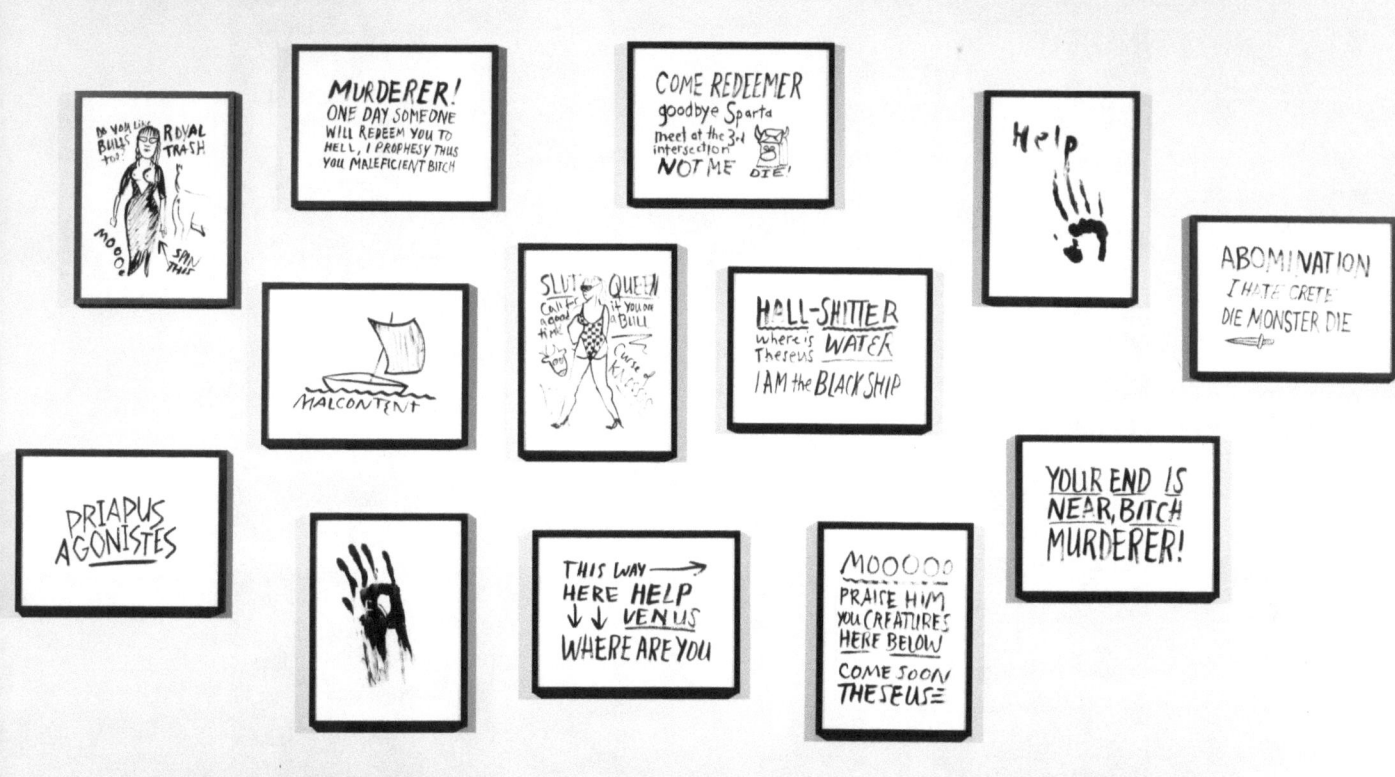

Pl. 15
Labyrinth Graffiti, 2013
Installation view, Samuel Dorsky Museum of Art
Ink on paper

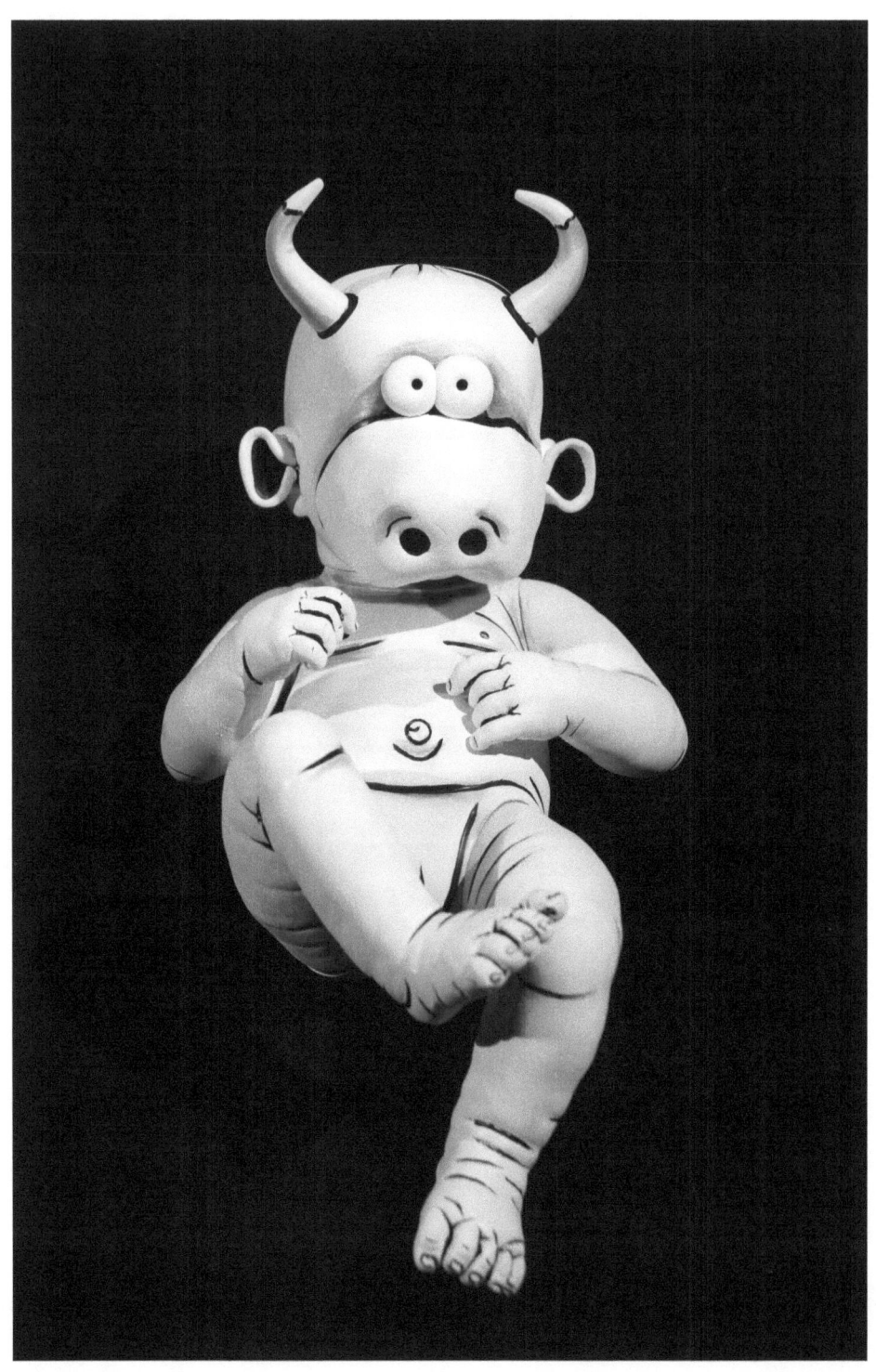

Pl. 16
Baby Minotaur, 2013
Plastic, polymer clay, and acrylic paint

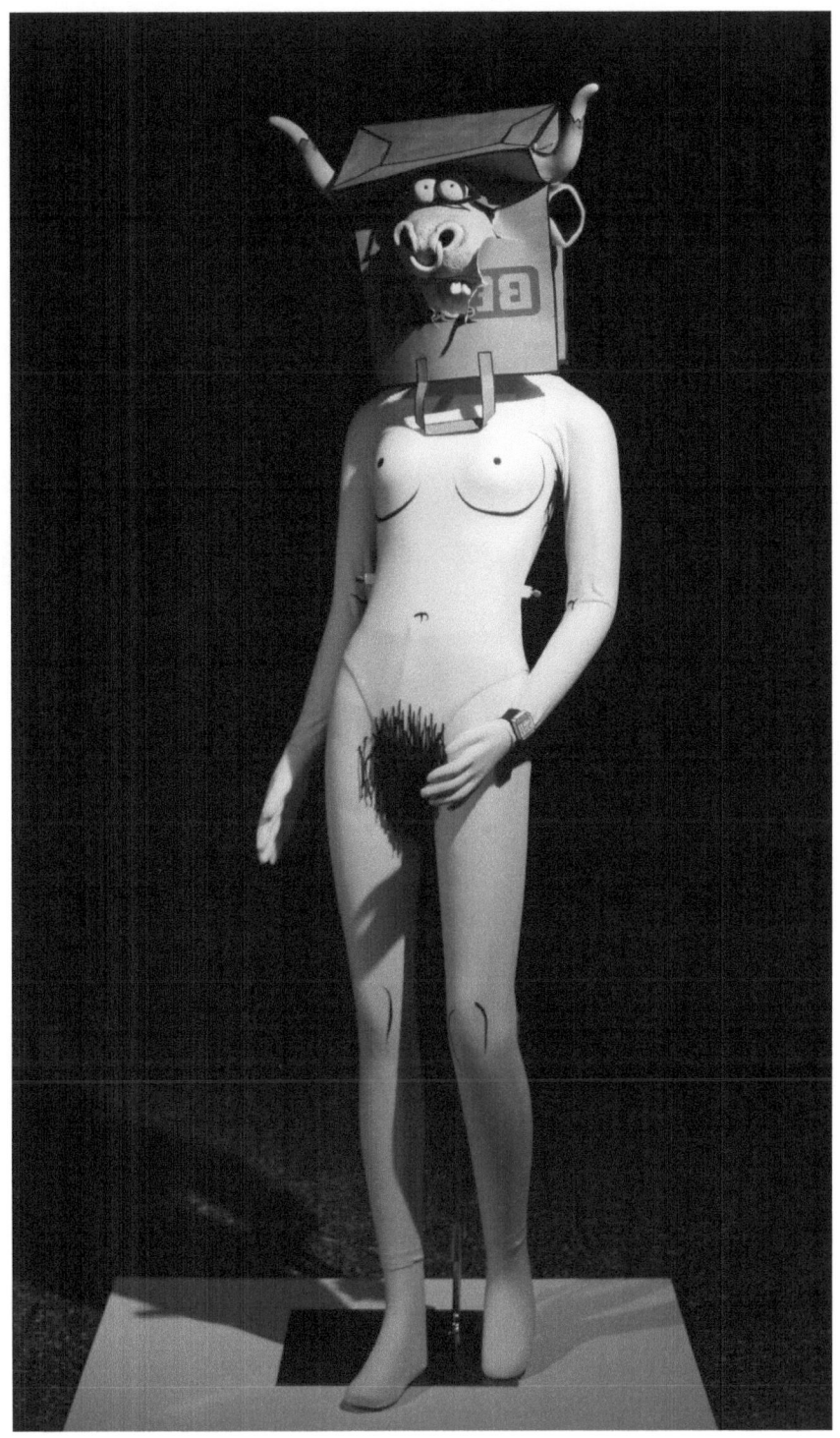

Pl. 17
Minotaur's Costume, 2013
Garment: fabric, acrylic paint, and yarn; Mask: neoprene, gesso, polymer clay, Stonehenge
paper, rubber, felt, and acrylic paint; Watch: elastic band, polymer clay, and acrylic paint

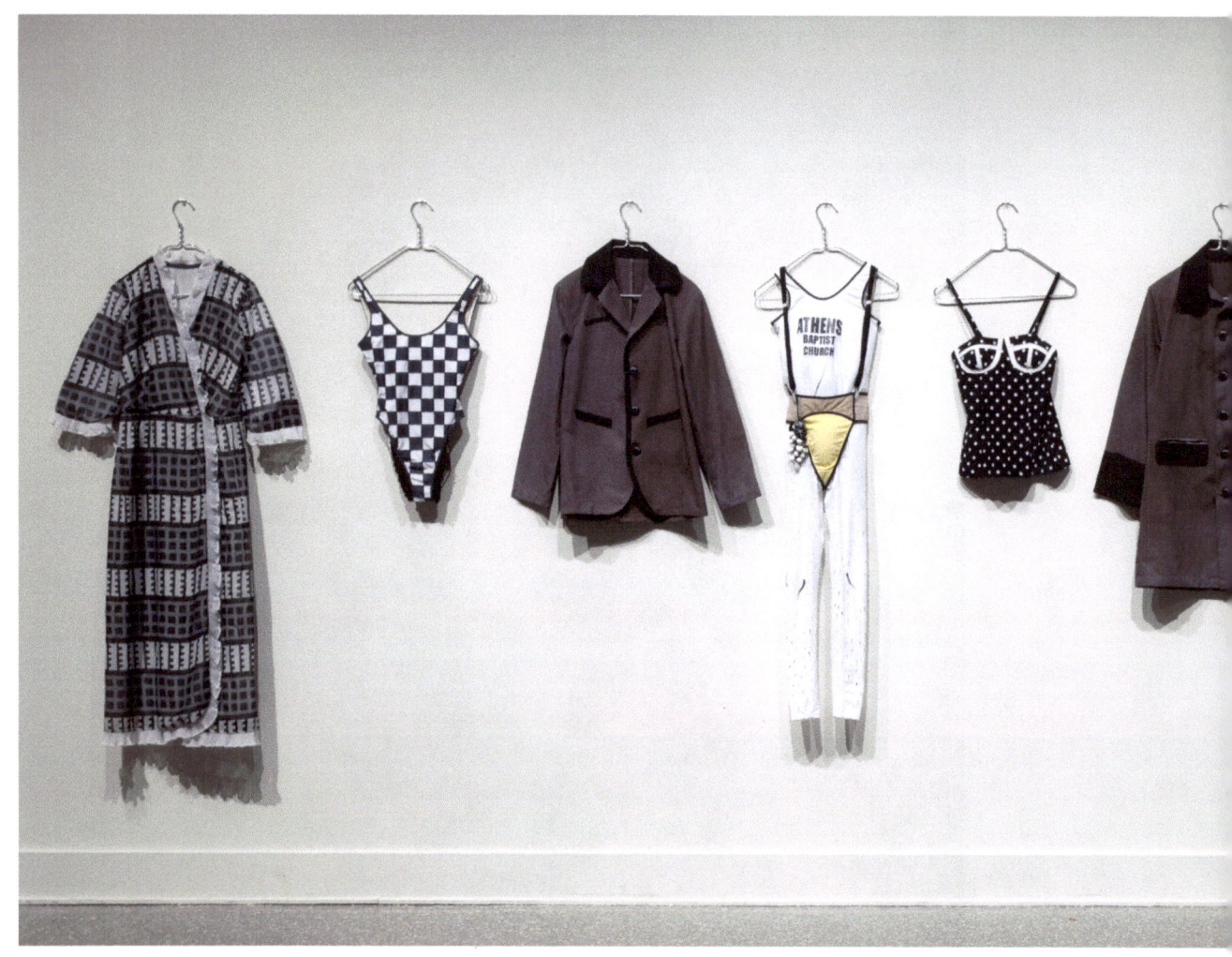

Pl. 18
LEFT TO RIGHT:
Charlotte Corday's Gown, 2011
Pasiphae's Swimsuit, 2013
Dandy's Coat 1, 2011
Priapus's Costume, 2013
Venus's Bustier, 2013
Dandy's Coat 2, 2011
Volleyball Player (Nude), 2013
Soldier's Uniform, 2010
Miss Spelt's Costume, 2013
Dandy's Coat 3, 2011
Sisyphus's Straightjacket, 2011
Installation view, Samuel Dorsky Museum of Art
Mixed media

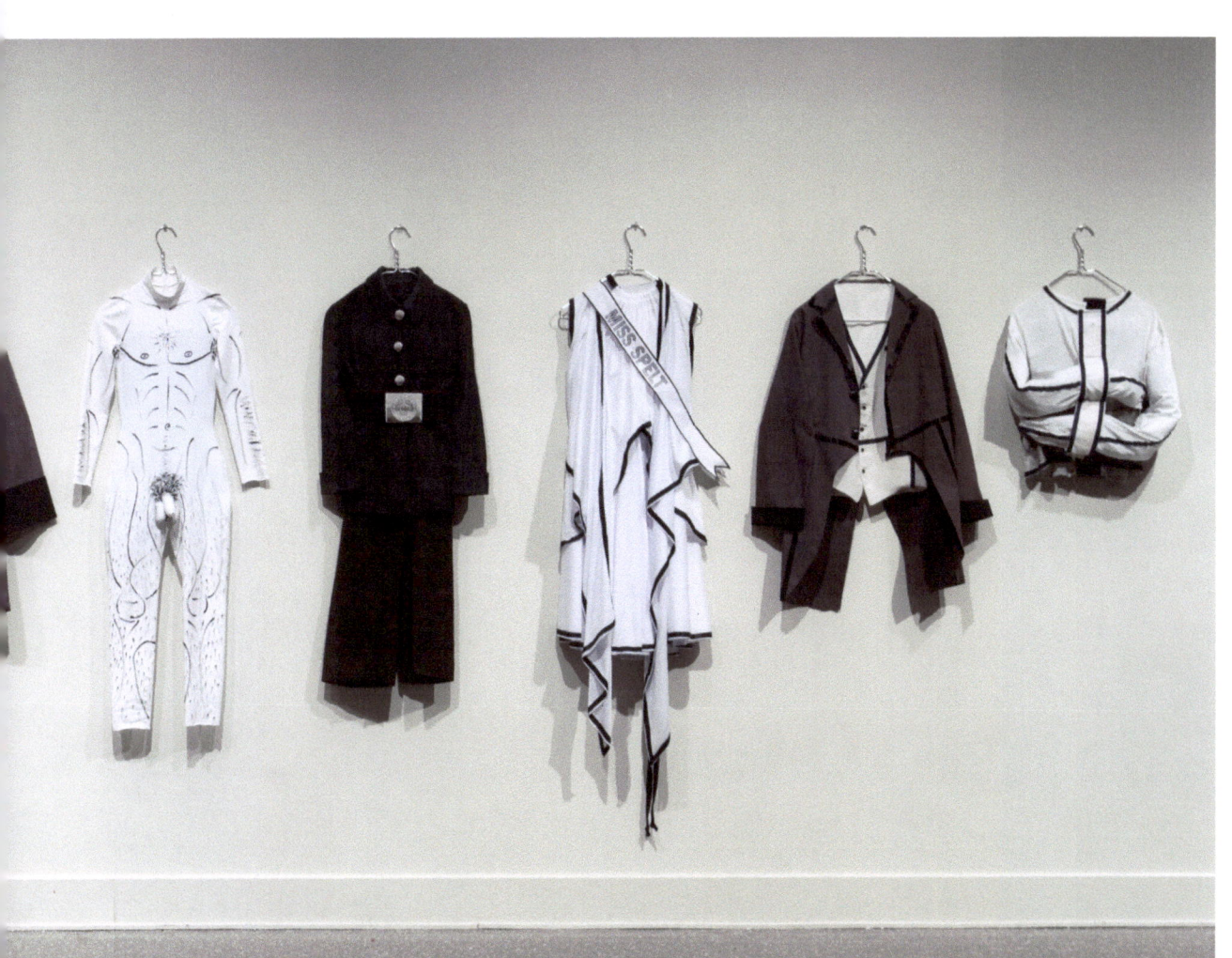

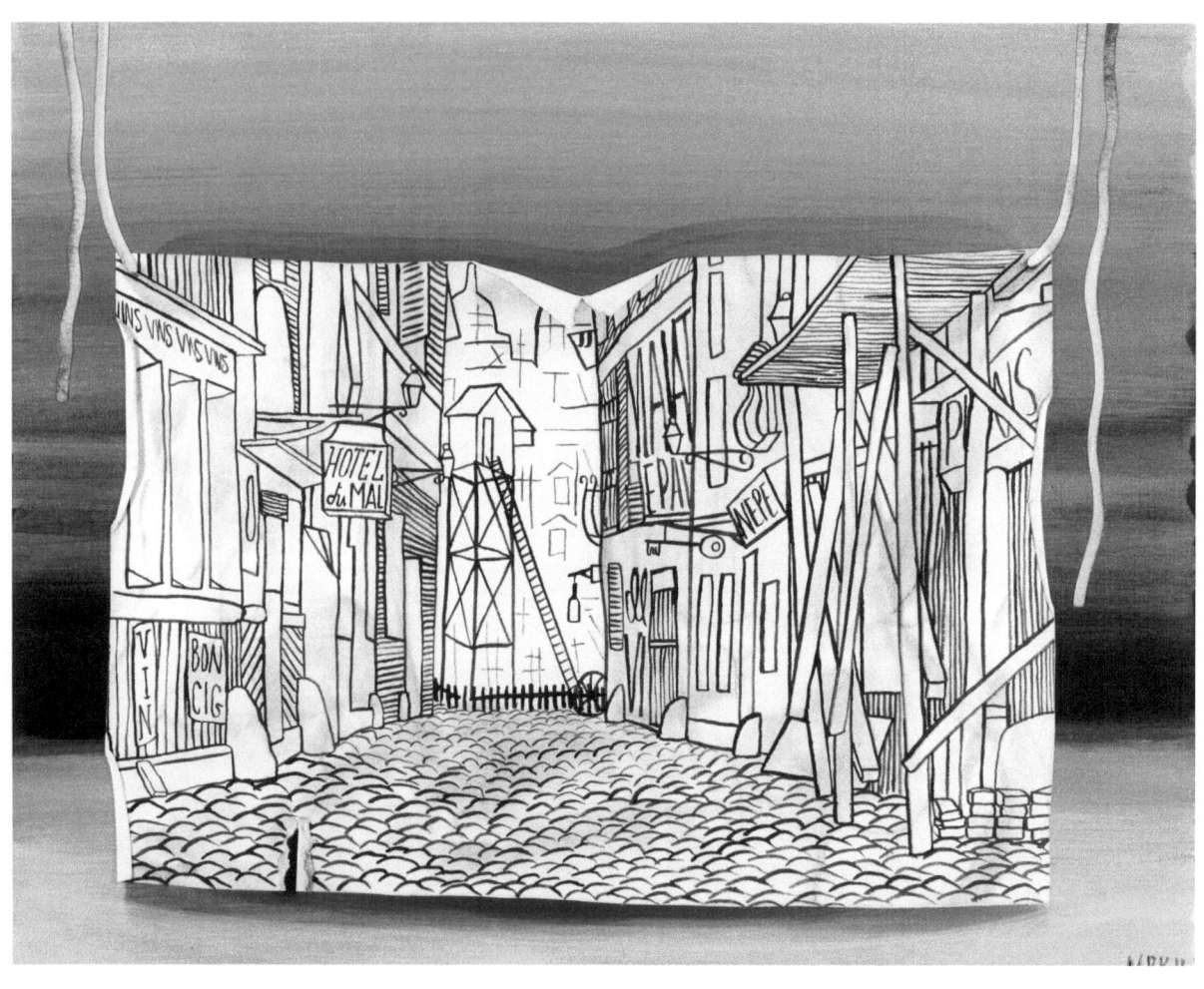

Pl. 19
Haussmann's Slum, 2011
Collage, acrylic paint, ink, and charcoal on paper

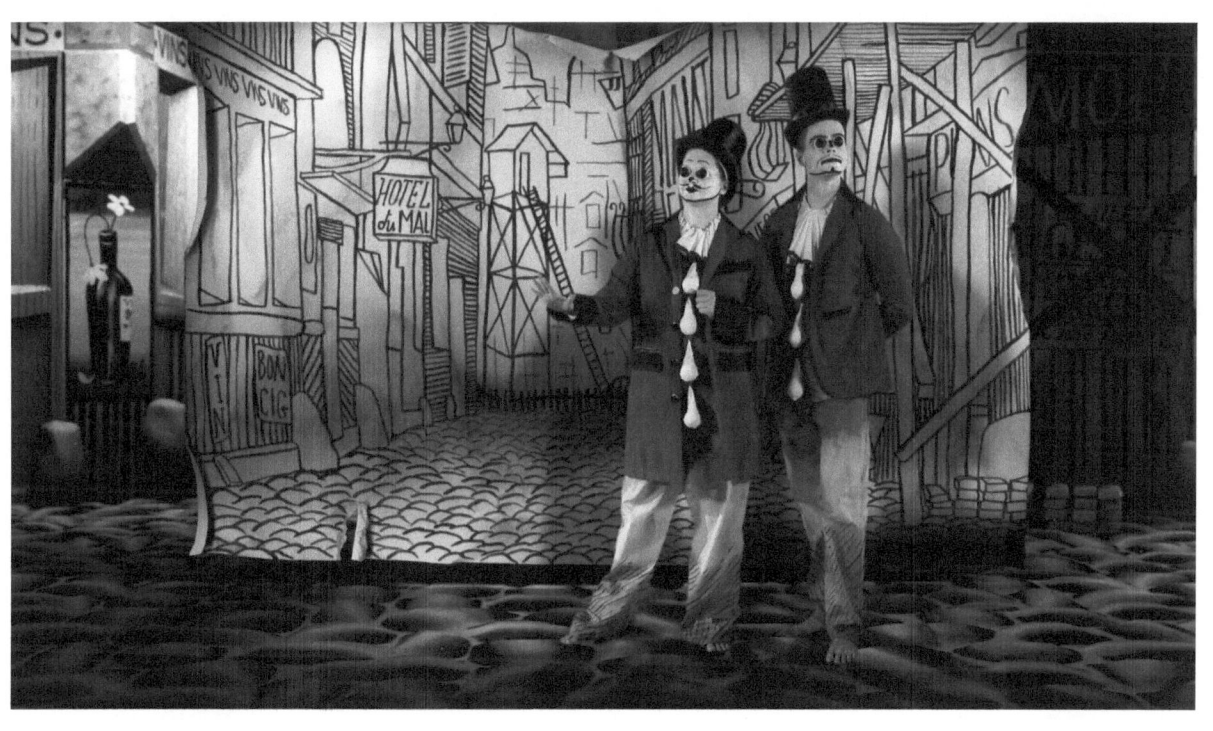

Pl. 20
The Syphilis of Sisyphus, 2011
Video still

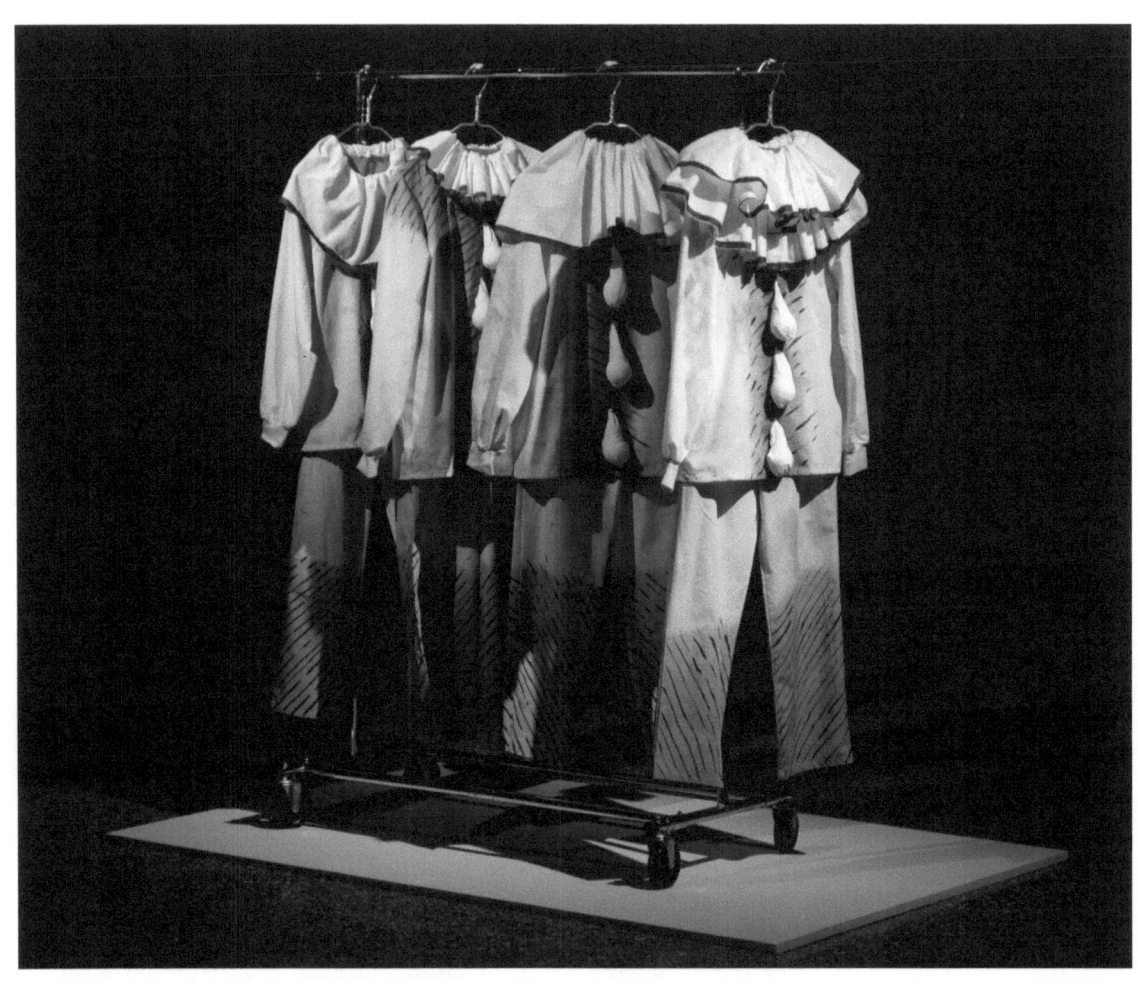

Pl. 21
Saltimbanques' Costumes, 2011
Installation view, Samuel Dorsky Museum of Art
Cotton, Styrofoam, thread, ribbon, and acrylic paint

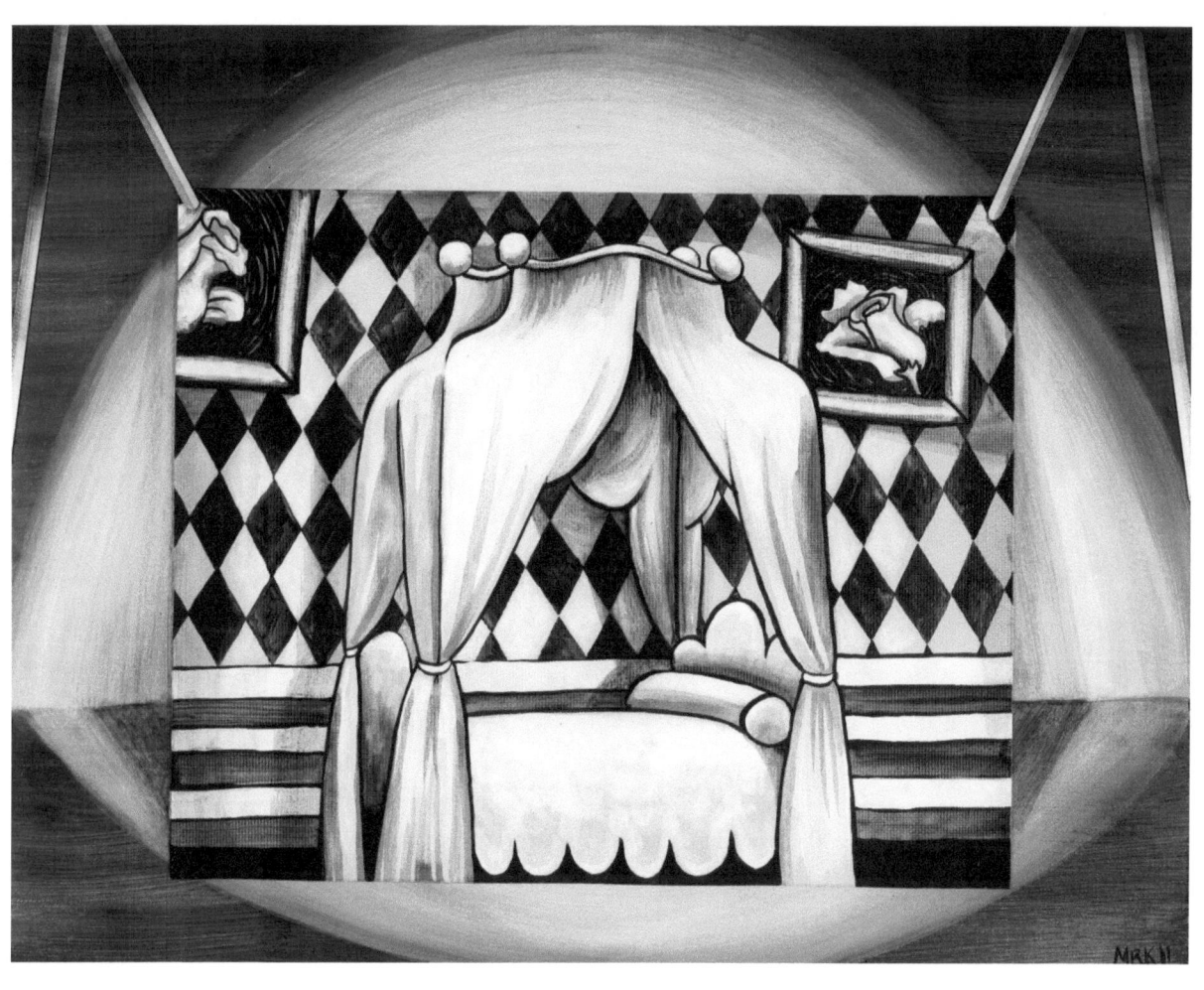

Pl. 22
Marie Antoinette's Bed, 2011
Collage and acrylic paint on paper

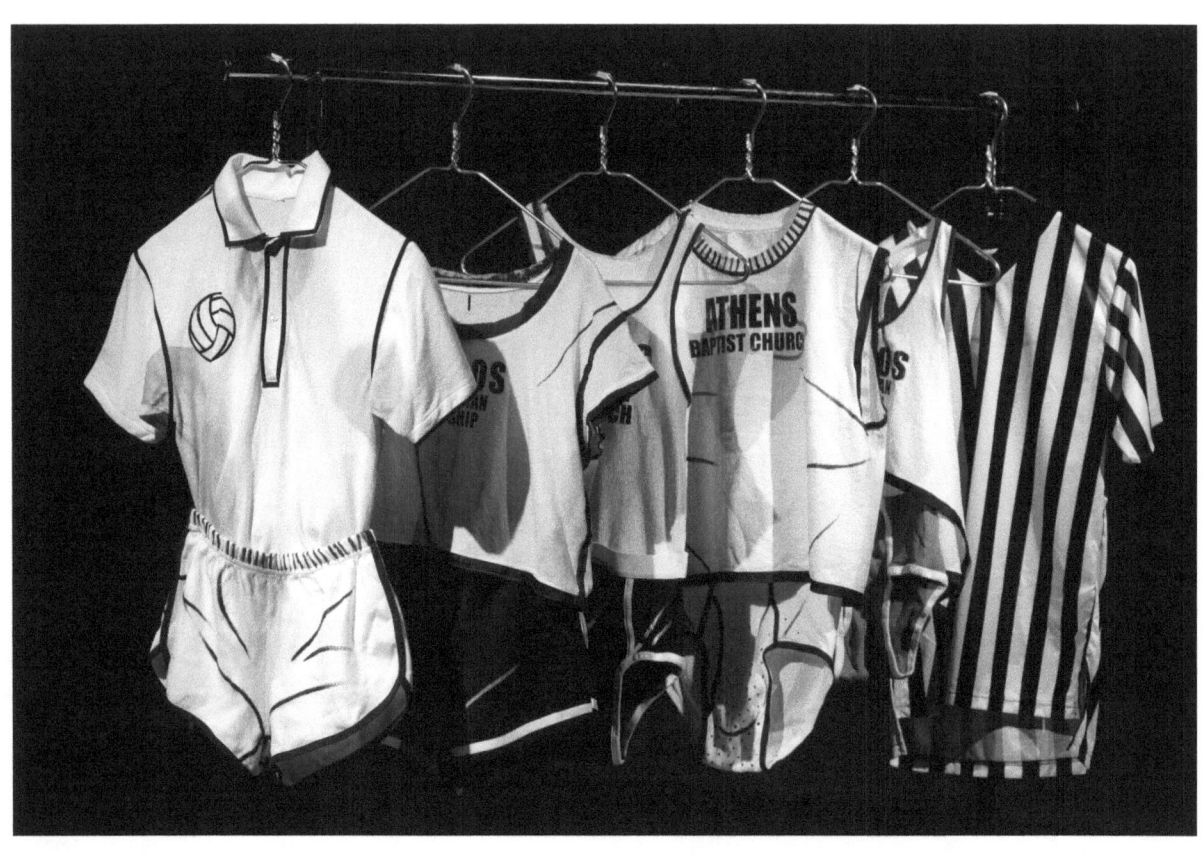

Pl. 23
Volleyball Players' Uniforms
Installation view, Samuel Dorsky Museum of Art
Mixed media

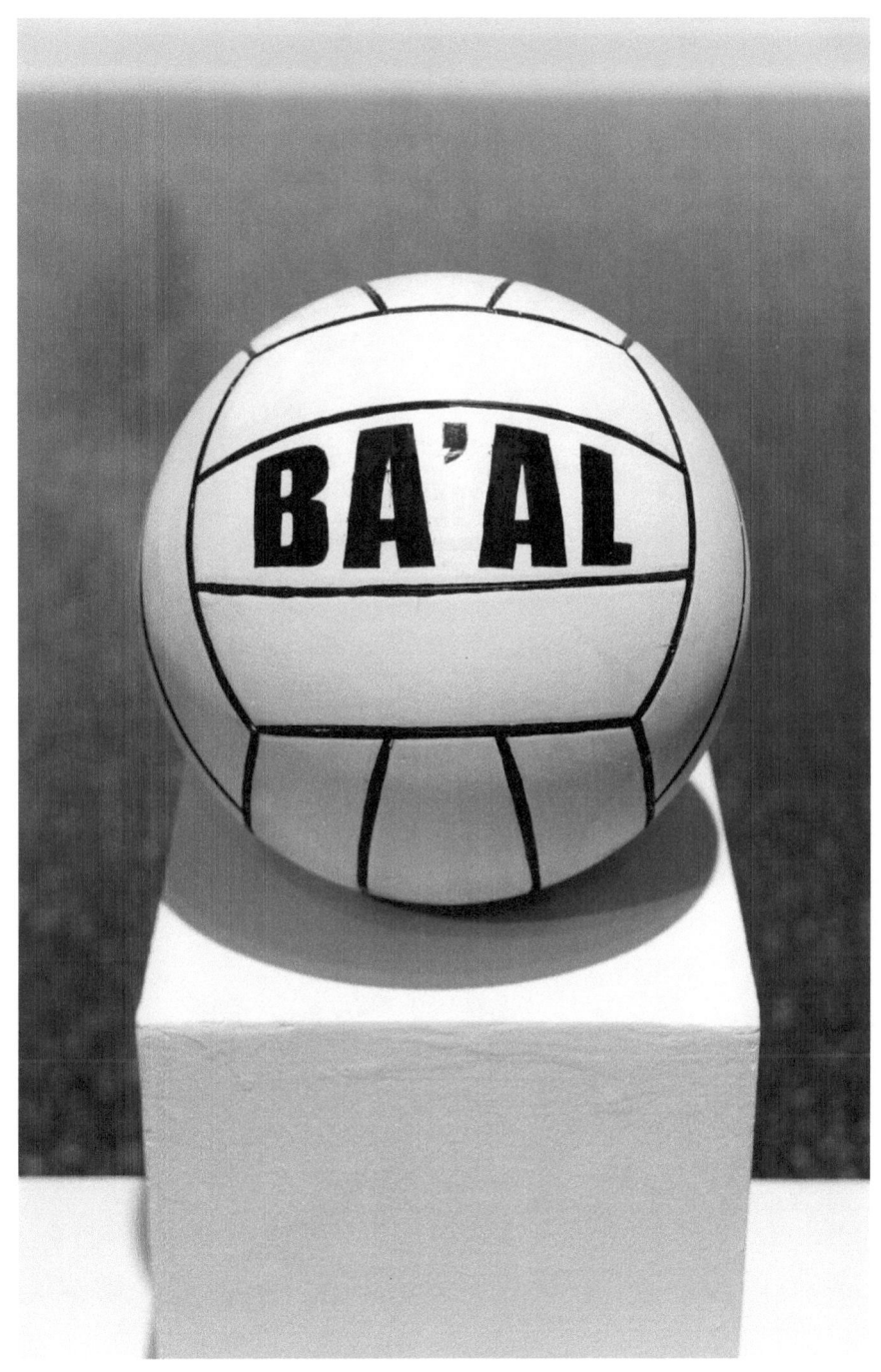

Pl. 24
Volleyball (Ba'al), 2013
Volleyball and acrylic paint

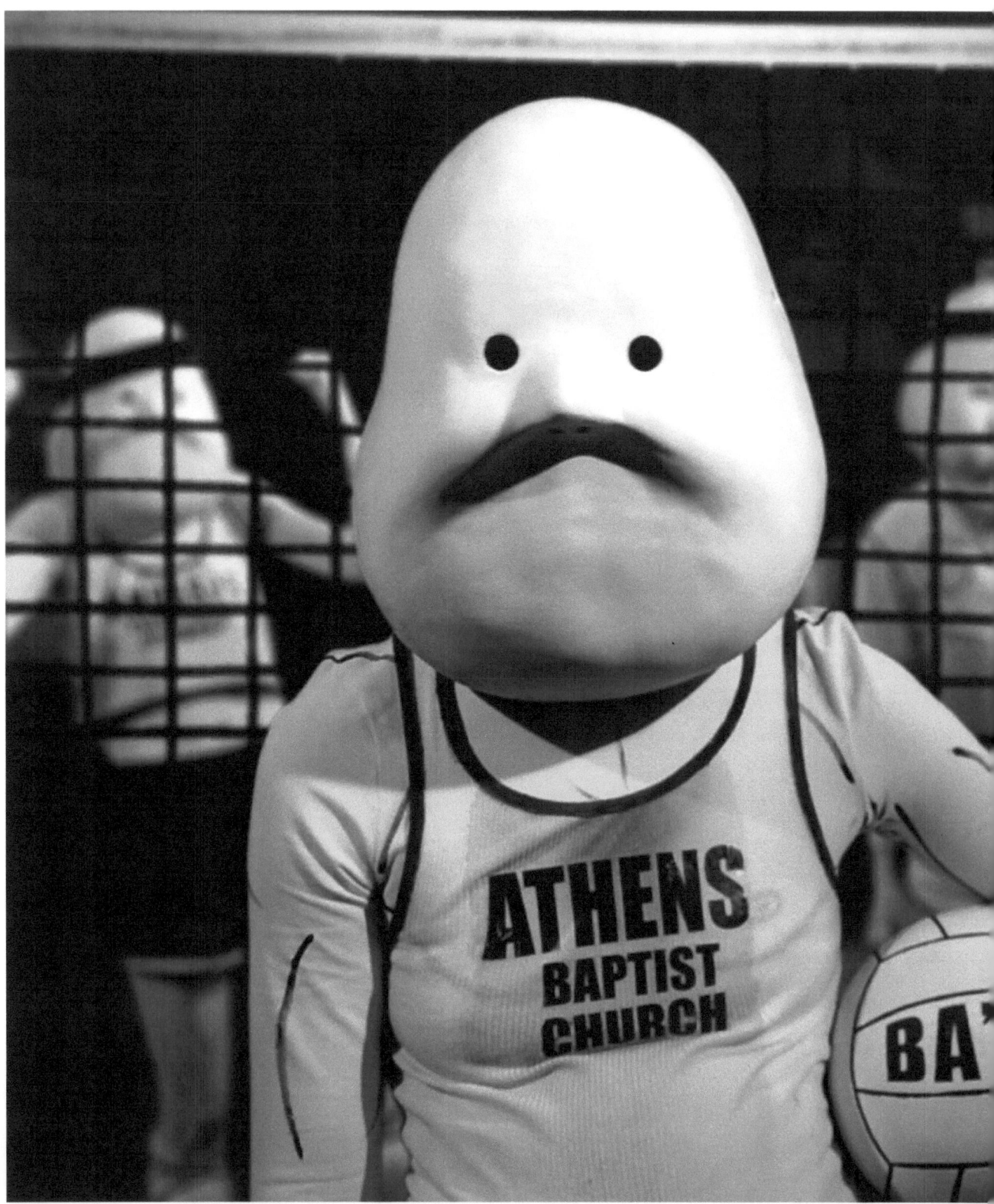

Pl. 25 *Priapus Agonistes*, 2013, video still

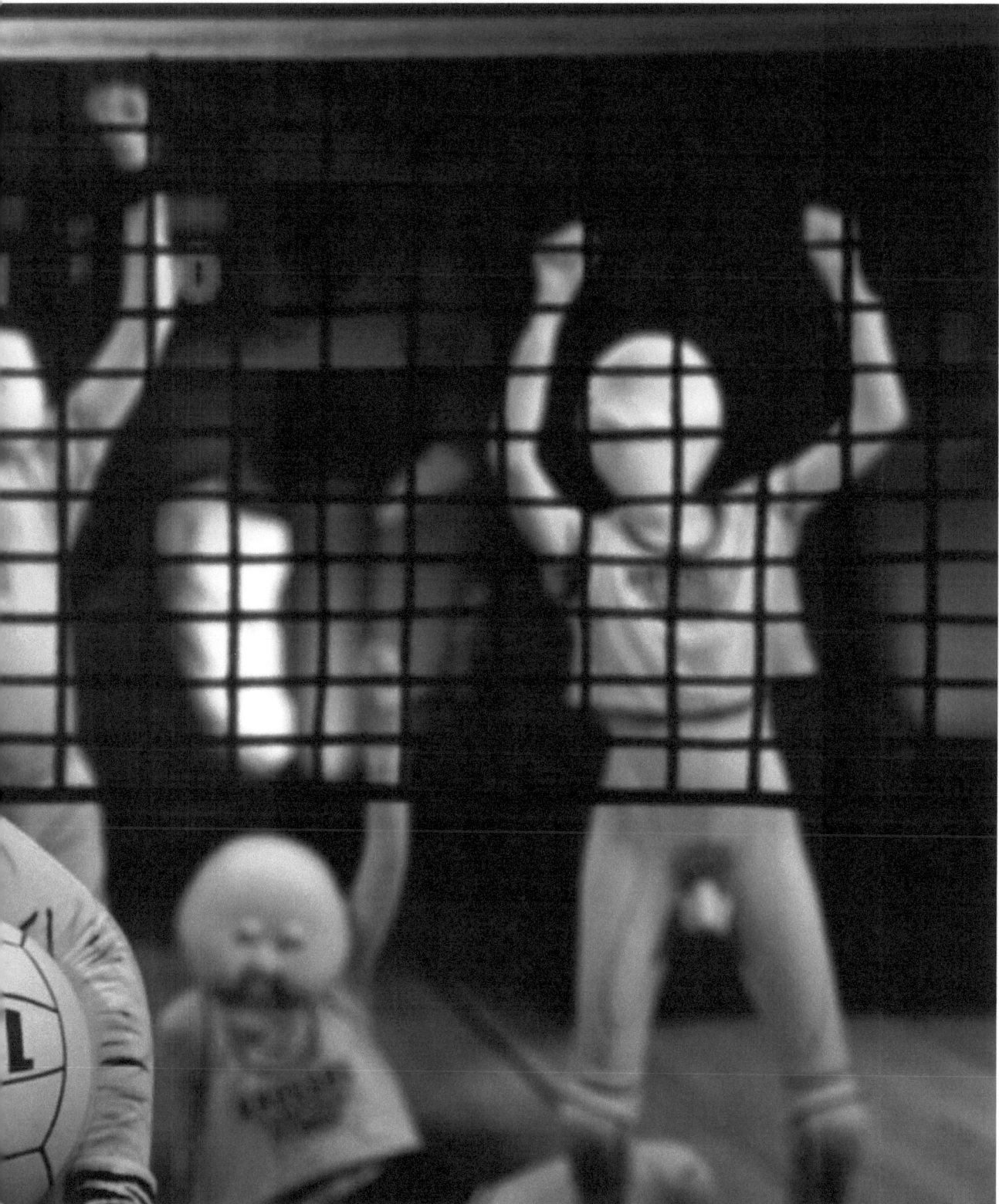

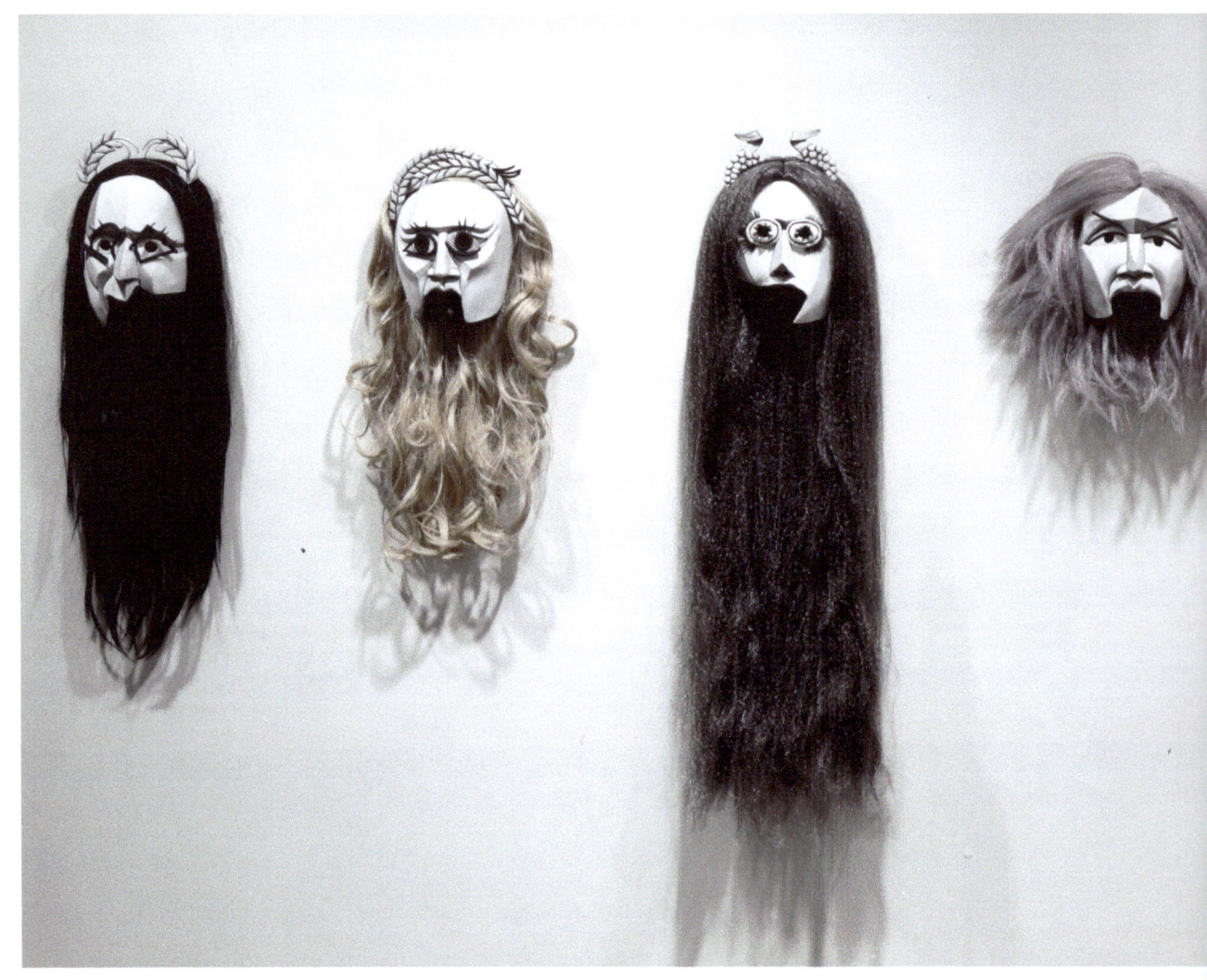

Pl. 26
Miss Barley's Mask, 2013
Miss Spelt's Mask, 2013
Miss Millet's Mask, 2013
Volleyball Player's Mask, 2013
Midwife's Mask, 2013
Ariadne's Mask, 2013
Daedalus's Mask, 2013
Venus's Mask, 2013
Installation view, Samuel Dorsky Museum of Art
Mixed media

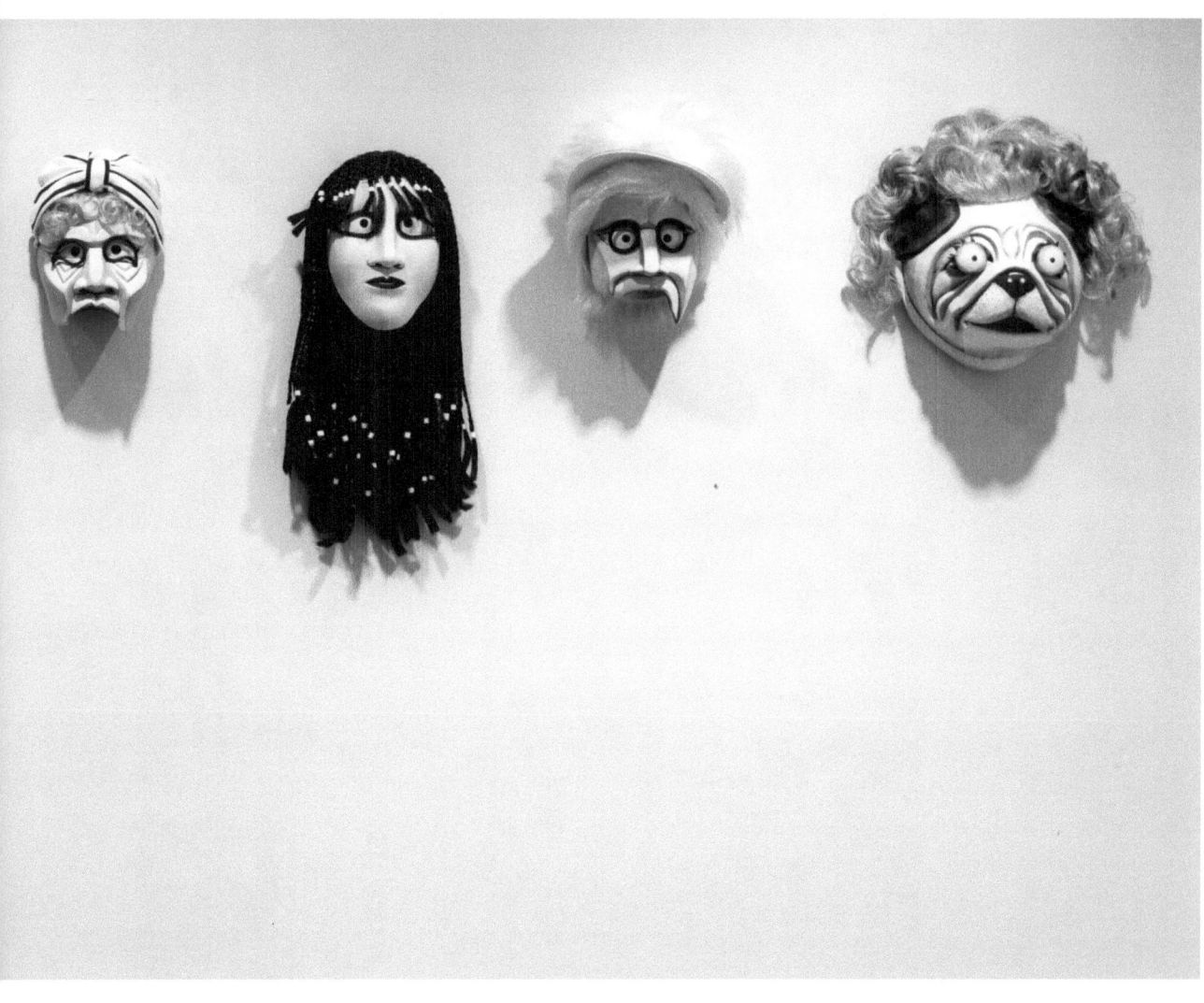

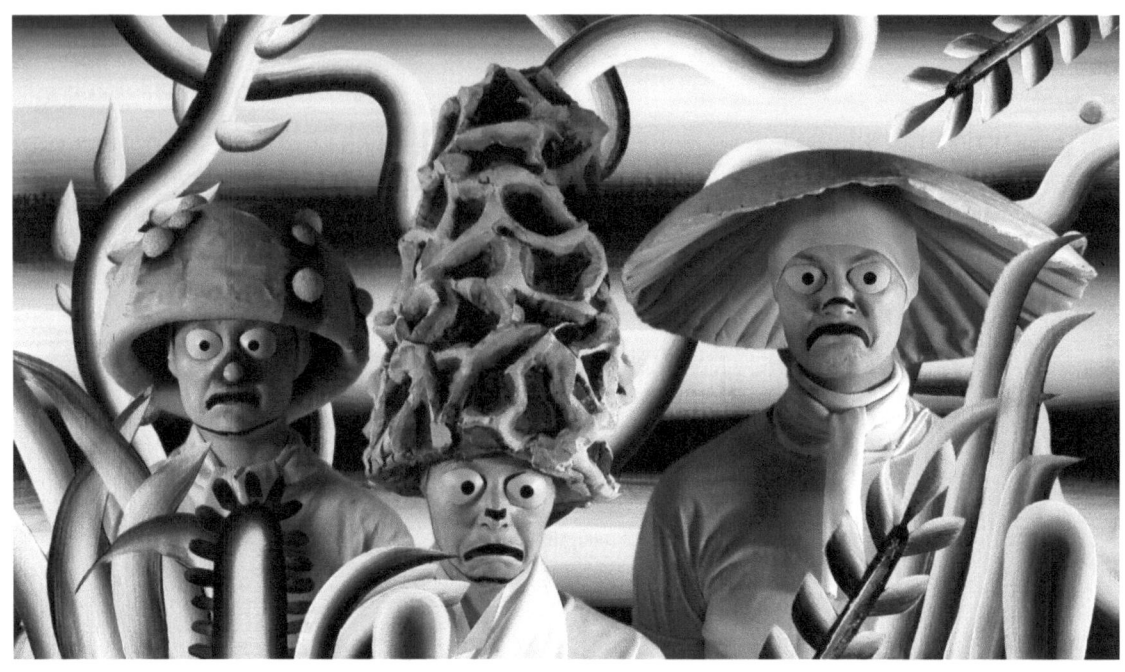

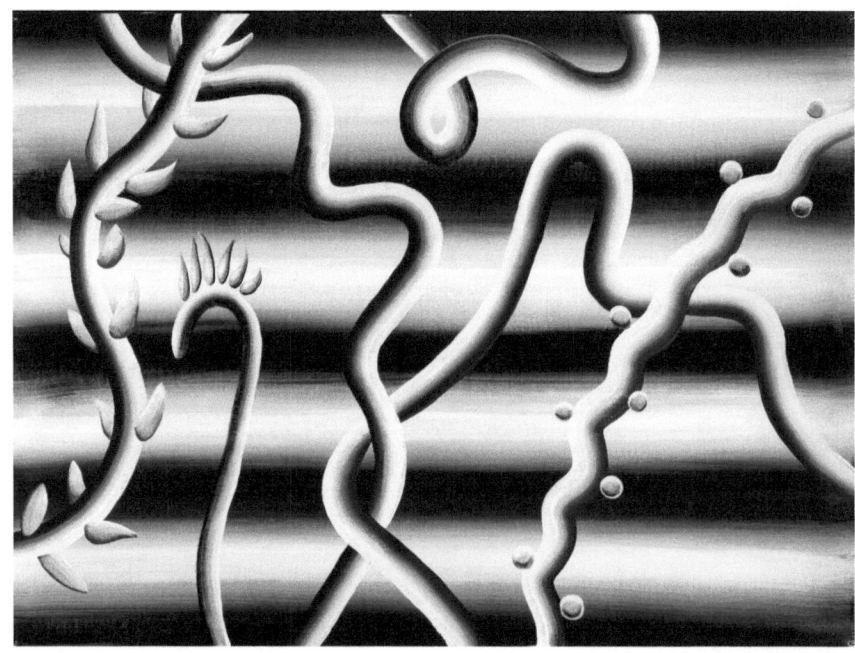

Pl. 27
The Syphilis of Sisyphus,
2011
Video still

Pl. 28
Mushroom Background,
2011
Acrylic paint on paper

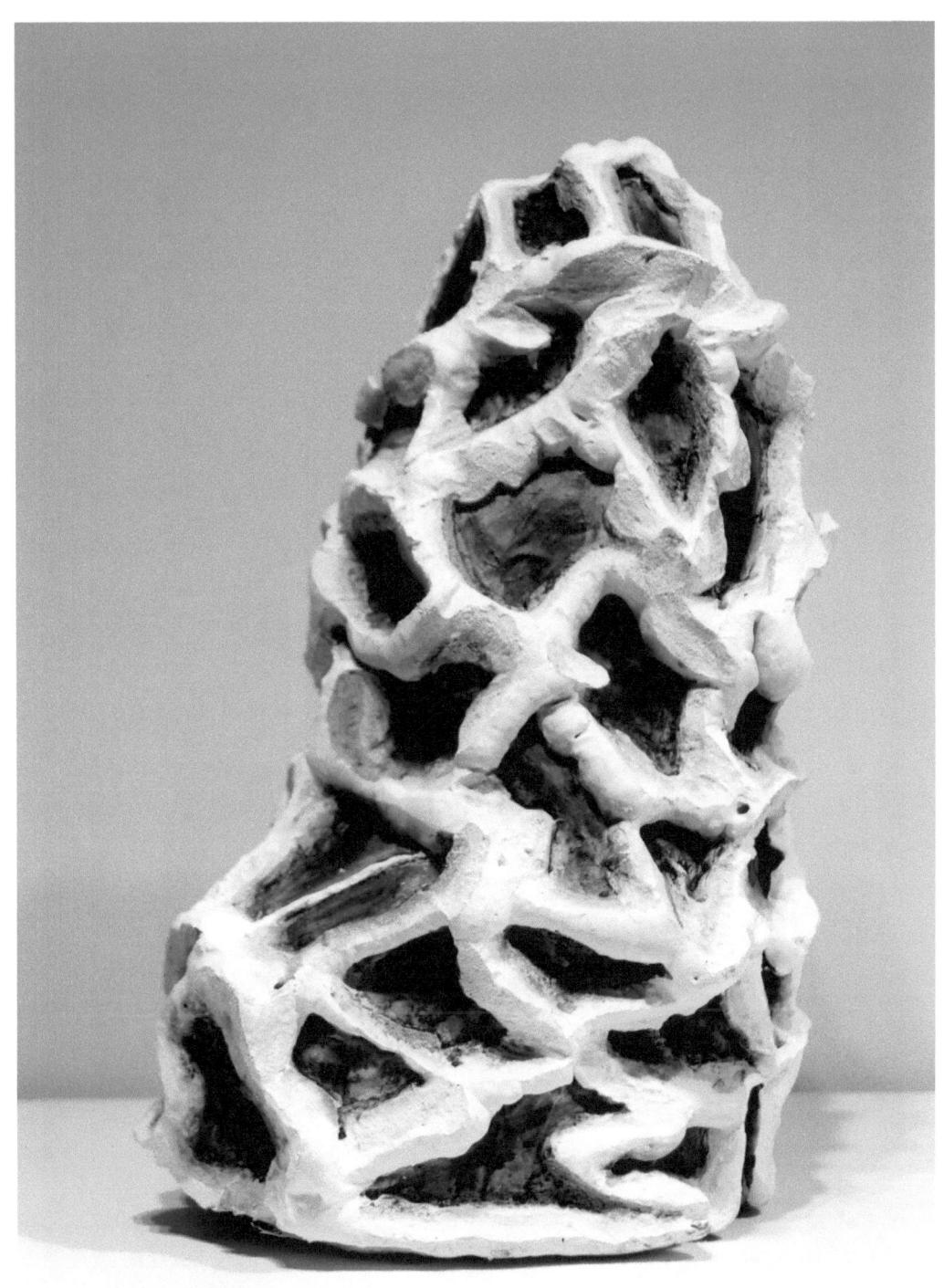

Pl. 29
Morel Hat, 2011
Insulating foam sealant, wire,
papier-mâché, and acrylic paint

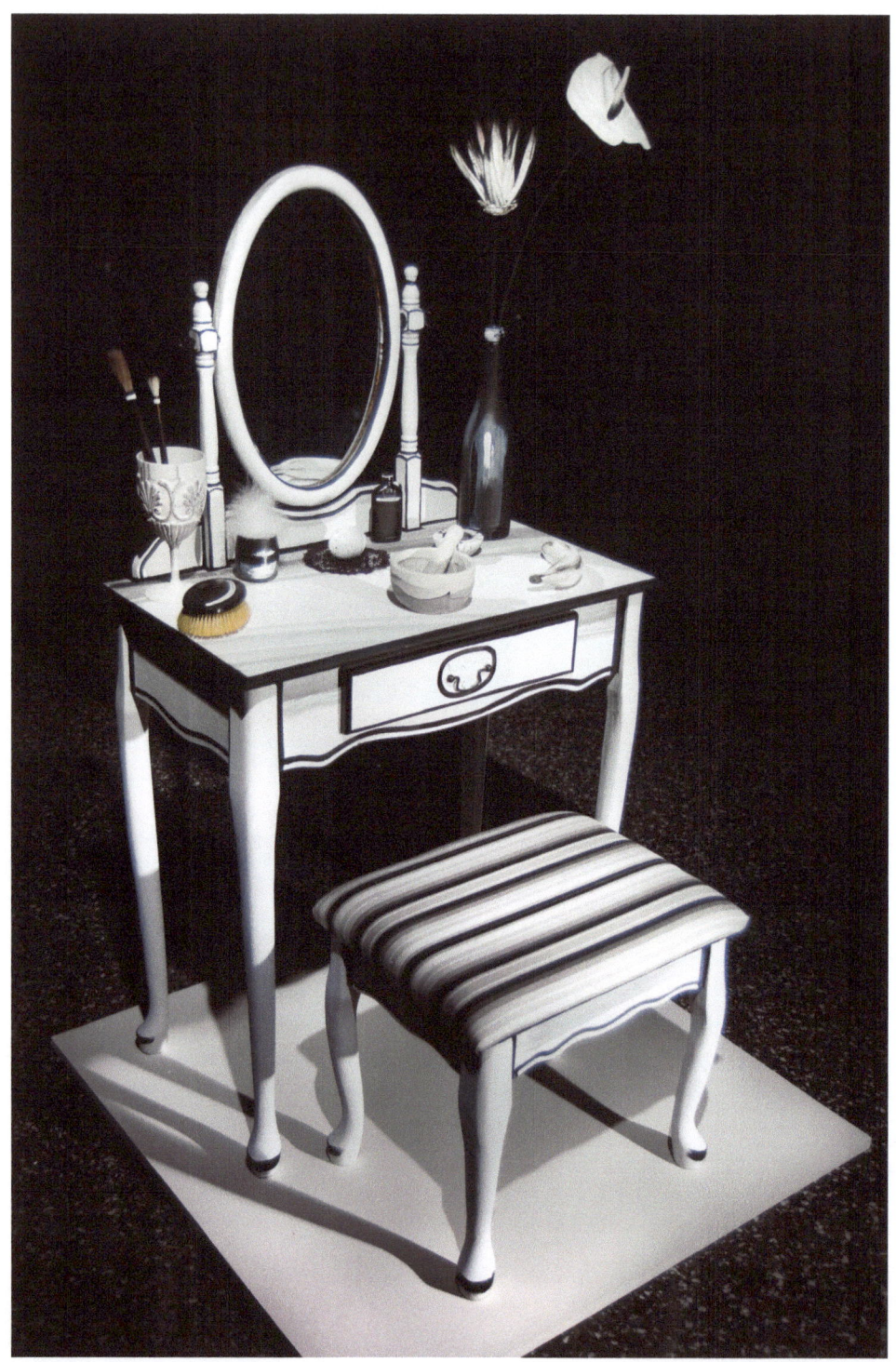

Pl. 30
Sisyphus's Vanity and Stool, 2011
Installation view, Samuel Dorsky Museum of Art
Mixed media

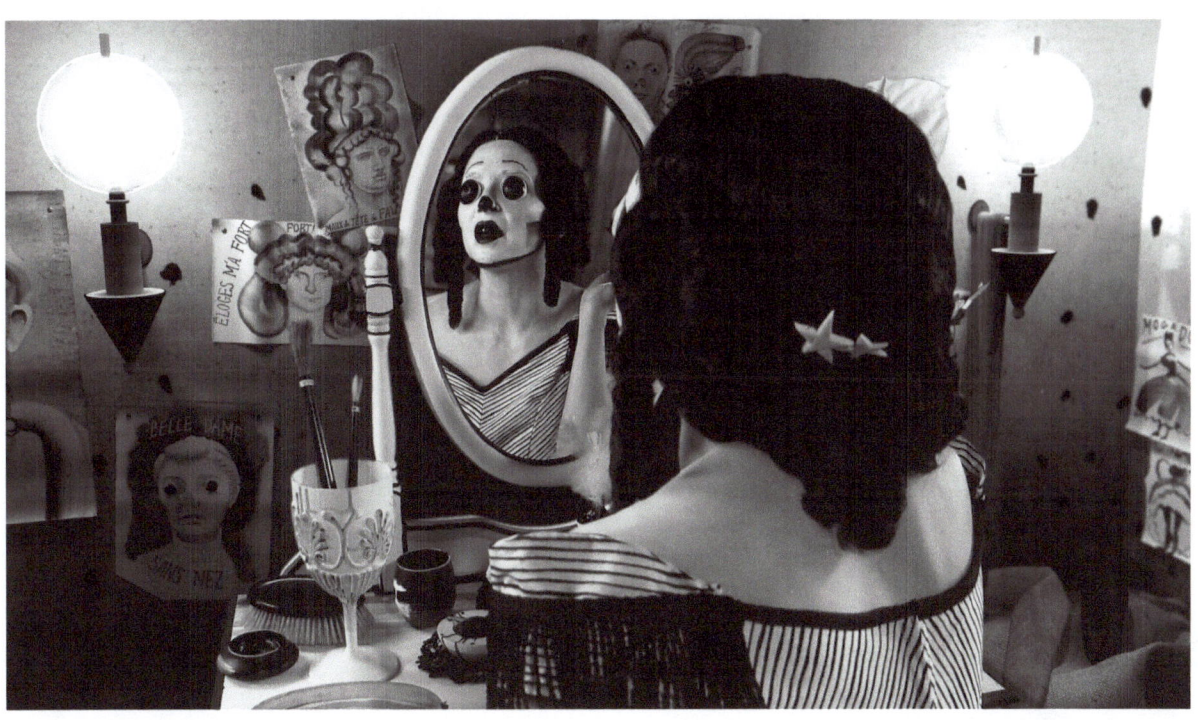

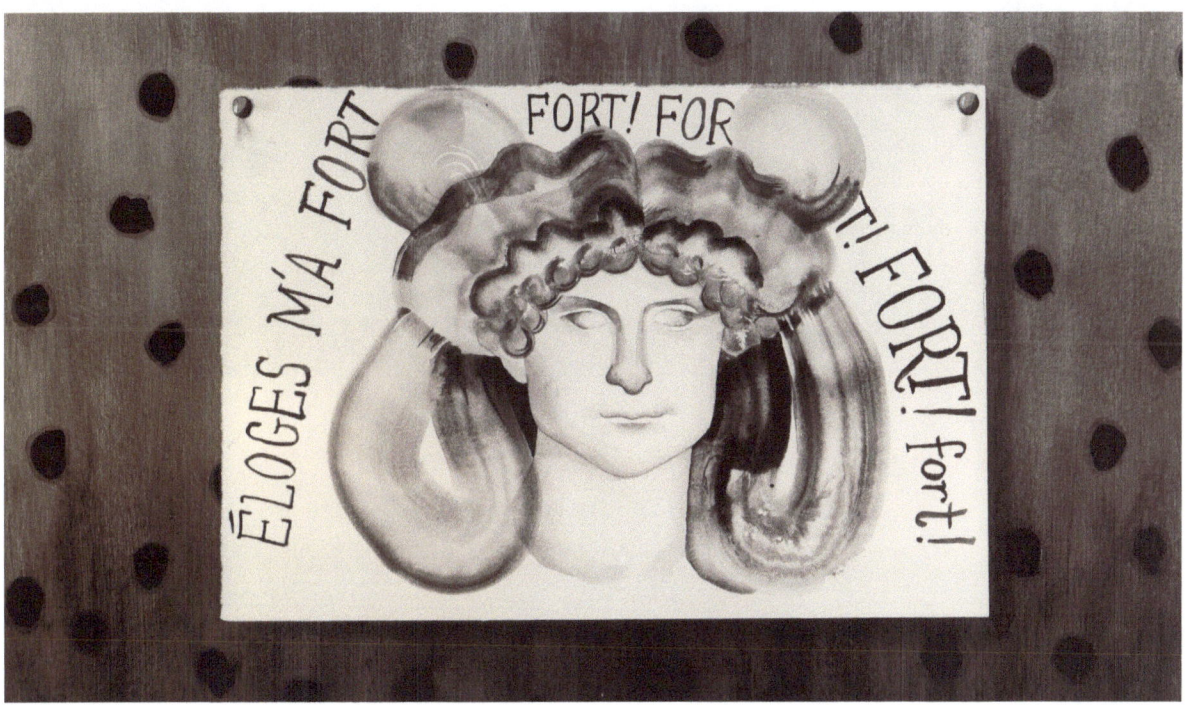

Pl. 31
The Syphilis of Sisyphus, 2011
Video still

Pl. 32
Fort! Fort!, 2011
Collage, watercolor, and acrylic paint on paper

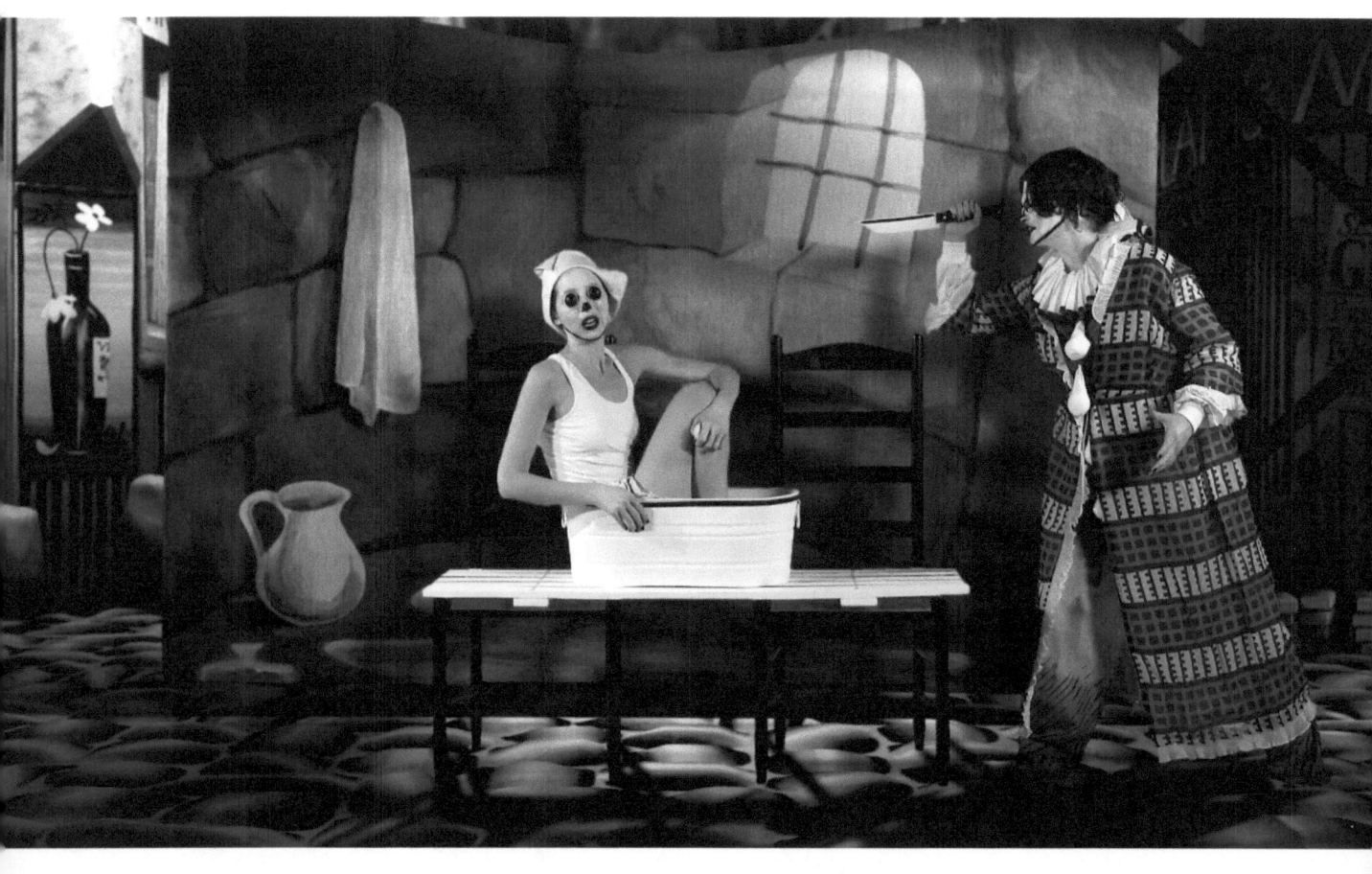

The Syphilis of Sisyphus, 2011
Video still

INTERVIEW WITH MARY REID KELLEY AND PATRICK KELLEY

By Corinna Ripps Schaming

Corinna Ripps Schaming
Most artists who work collaboratively talk about how much the work evolves out of that collaboration. How does the collaboration process work for you?

Patrick Kelley
We've only made six videos. In terms of how we work together, that means that a lot changes between them.

Mary Reid Kelley
One of the best parts of working on your sixth or seventh film, rather than on your second, is that you've developed a shorthand of words together. I think we both understand equally the emotional feeling and the visual quality that we want the work to have. Of course we talk about it, and we adjust it in real time, but we've gained a co-knowledge of what we need and what we want. Another benefit of this shared knowledge is that we can work more independently, so at many points in the process we're "working alone together." I do all the writing and the research myself, but I'm constantly talking to Pat about what I'm reading and writing.

CRS
Do you think of the writing in terms of verse or as a screenplay?

MRK
Now that we've made a half-dozen films together, I've definitely started to think of them more as scripts and screenplays, although the initial works were more like recitations of a poem. The project becomes collaborative when it stops becoming notes and words on paper and starts becoming a film. Probably the

part of our process that conforms to most people's ideal of collaboration—sitting knee to knee and forehead to forehead, making decisions—is storyboarding, deciding who comes in from the left and who needs to get hit by something coming in from the right. We do that together. We also edit together. After the filming is done, that's when Pat does a lot of his work on the digital sets alone, but beforehand we talk about what the set should generally look like and then he builds it, and then I try to leave him alone and not breathe over his shoulder.

PK

Our very first film, *Camel Toe*—you can't really call it a film. It's ninety seconds of recitation. Mary had written a poem about an airman from World War I, which came out of her working with so many text paintings, literally painting texts and poems. It became this natural thing—I was visiting and had the camera, so she had the idea to make herself up to look like a cartoon version of the airman à la Snoopy and recite her poem. All very simple...from there, things have grown increasingly more complex.

CRS

Mary, you've said that working in video has allowed you to make the paintings you always wanted to make. How so?

MRK

All kinds of different paintings go into the videos or are tangential to them. There's painting upon an actual object—for example, the globe in *The Syphilis of Sisyphus*, which is Diderot's prop in the video. We bought it at Target or some-where and spray-painted it. We deleted most of the information on the mapping part of the globe and redrew a kind of cartoon version over it.

A lot of the painting I do is "painting out" or redaction, removing the visual information native to the object and replacing it with a graphic representation. Some of the painting is pattern mimesis—imitating wood grain, or marble, or cobblestones. Pat and I had to figure out the cobblestones in the *Sisyphus* street set together, because my painted pattern was destined to become wallpapered on the 3-D structure of the bumpy stones, so the drawing and the digital structure had to be built in tandem. After the film is finished, I make paintings of the characters themselves, which is a chance to explicate the different redactions and contradictions of image that define the characters—like painting my own jawline alongside the jawline I drew over it, or replacing flesh tones with white clown paint, or taking out an eye and putting in a picture of the eye.

CRS

And your earlier work—before *Camel Toe*—what kinds of things were you doing then?

MRK

In one of my earlier series I made re-creations of photographs from the Civil War. I'm from South Carolina, and my eighth-grade textbook referred to the Civil War as the "war of Southern Independence." For me, growing up with liberal parents in the South meant an early awareness of complexity and contradictions in the historical record, but also a more primal feeling of belonging to that ugliness whether I liked it or not.

And since the Civil War coincided with the beginning of photography, and that photographic record has its own complex ethical landscape, it was very fascinating to me. I made dolls that looked like historic characters from particular photographs—Abraham Lincoln, Frederick Douglass, Julia Ward Howe. Then Pat would photograph the dolls, and then I would adjust that image with paint, similar to the 'retouching' of photography that was common in that era. At that point, I was trying to figure out how to represent the gaps between the historical character, the photographs themselves, and my artificial constructions.

CRS

Were you doing this as a graduate student?

MRK

No, before I went to graduate school but after undergraduate.

CRS

So you've always worked in this kind of hybrid way, with one foot in the real world and the other in an artificial, symbolic world?

MRK

Well, I've always felt that I could easily mimic something, which is a good tactic for jumping between the two. For example, if I had a photograph of Lincoln, I could easily replicate his face in that photograph with modeling clay and felt and hot glue. And now when I perform as these characters, I think of them as containers for ideology in much the same way that Lincoln, the historical person, has become eclipsed by his own rich symbolism: he's in films, he's on currency. I want my characters to function in the same way: as symbols—the "back-of-the-dime" Lincoln, not the Doris Kearns Goodwin biographical Lincoln.

CRS

The type of stylization or abstraction that your characters undergo also occurs in your choice of language for each video work. Would you say that's the place where everything intersects for you?

MRK

Definitely. There's a vast difference between the formality of verse and living speech—between the moment-to-moment conversation of a person, and the artifice of poetry. And there's an analogy between that difference and the difference between a living person and a cartoon image of that same individual. I think those artificial worlds, which are the worlds of videos, are so compelling because even though they're both so formalized and stylized, they can describe something about being human that realism can't fully capture, no matter how much detail you have.

CRS
How did your interest in history and literature enter the mix?

MRK
I feel as though my interest in history and my interest in literature are separate from my own long-standing interest in art and in thinking of myself as an artist... I was one of those kids who always felt like I was an artist, it was "my thing." I loved to read, but it was separate from art. It wasn't until I started working in video that I started pulling my other interests into my artwork. I didn't set out to make videos, but ultimately I found the form irresistible—the potential of a narrative form, an expansive form. I could finally see the figures I wanted to paint, but I didn't see them until I had heard them and started writing in their voices. Then I could draw on history in general, and my own history. This was all new to me. Once I started to write and make videos, I could draw on all this stuff that I didn't know I'd been storing up for years!

CRS
So there was this moment when you realized, "I can do this, I don't need permission, I'm just going to do it." And you started to push out and find meaningful ways to contain all these interests and ideas that were significant to you by extending your practice beyond painting in the conventional sense.

MRK
Maybe other people can contain the whole broad expanse of what they can possibly express in a painting, but I can't [laughs]...so that's why you have these videos.

CRS
You've said that the installation of your videos is very important to you because through installation you can provide a collective experience for your audience. Lots of people can watch them together, and watch them over and over, and if one person laughs, another can respond to the laughter. And the idea of stylization or abstraction also plays into how your videos are experienced; for example, you deliberately use clichés or archetypes. Are you hoping that these vehicles will bring points of recognition for people collectively as they experience your work?

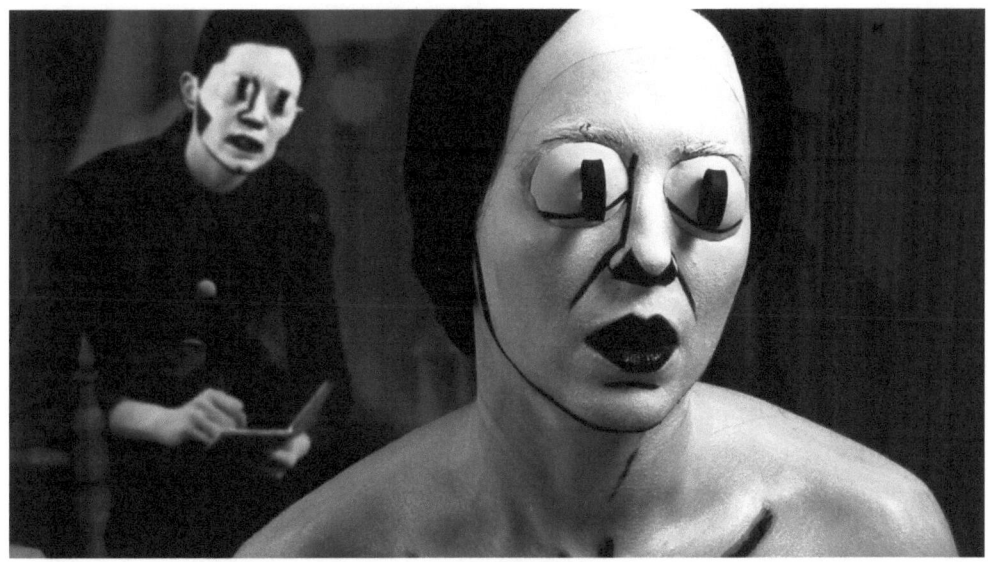

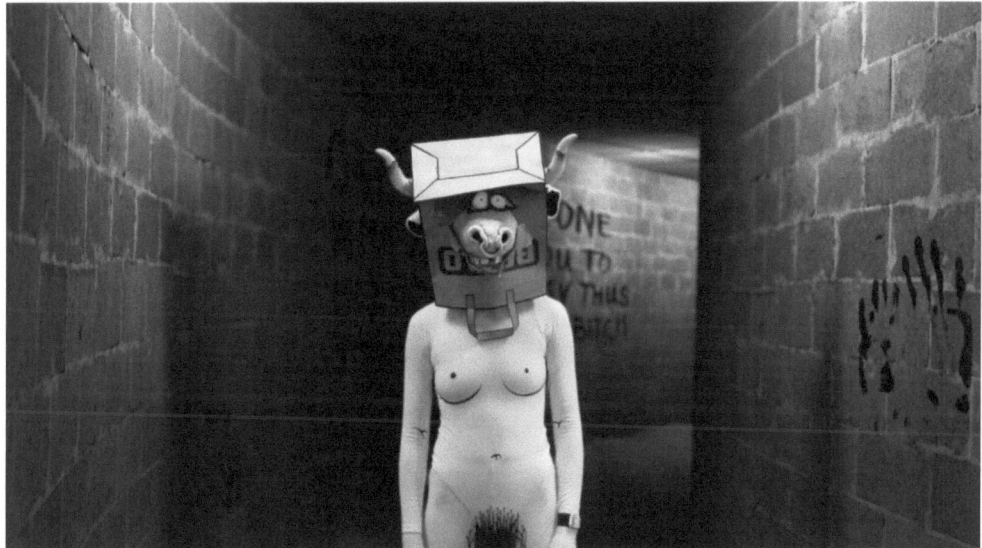

You Make Me Iliad, 2010
Video still

Priapus Agonistes, 2013
Video still

MRK

Well, I think what I was saying in terms of the symbolism that results from redactions, whether they're done to a face or through the formalization of speech and verse—I think the extra thing, the extra quality that those redactions can give us as individuals, is a signpost toward our place in the collective. When I think about people watching the work, I want them to experience it collectively because I think that's a very different experience. This isn't something I realized while I was making the videos, it was something I began to notice afterwards when I was watching people watch the work. People were watching each other as much as they were watching the work, and that added to their experience. It wasn't a distraction at all...it was almost like an alchemy that I wasn't expecting. People just felt the work was funnier or more significant when they watched it with someone else, as part of a collective.

Active interpretation is so exquisite, and so intimate, but also frightening...it can be frightening to encounter something complex, and to know that the onus is on you to interpret it in real time. I know that's how people feel when they watch my videos, because that's how I feel when I see or read something complex. It's a pressure-filled situation. There's pressure on you as a viewer, like if you're watching *Hamlet* or something...there's pressure to engage adequately in that active interpretation.

CRS
I think that's one of the things that make your videos so successful. You allow for shared experience to happen, you're open to it. And it also plays into your decision to show working objects and source material in this exhibition and at your exhibition at the ICA in Boston. By revealing your sources and sharing the history of your process, are you consciously giving your audience more points of entry into the work?

MRK
One thing I always show as a preliminary to the World War I work—*Sadie, The Saddest Sadist* or *You Make Me Iliad,* is *The Wipers Times,* a trench magazine that was published during the war by a British engineering battalion. It's quite obscure, unfortunately, but it's so funny and bleak, full of puns and jokes. Absolutely black humor in that particular Anglo-Irish tradition that runs in a line from Jonathan Swift to Monty Python. *The Wipers Times* totally participates in that distinctive viewpoint. I don't think I would have been able to be as free with historical material if I hadn't discovered it. It's so incredibly heartbreaking to read about what happened during the war, and to realize the enormity of the casualties involved. *The Wipers Times* brought a critical viewpoint to the war through humor, one that proved that absurdity was the most logical response to an absurdly horrific war. The example was liberating to me.

CRS
I think some people are born with a deep desire to engage with history. It's either in your DNA, or it's not. When it's there, the obvious next step is to start delving more deeply into history the way that you do, through reading and research—going to that place where you can find alternate histories and then start to play with the official record. How do you sort through it all?

MRK

Historical artifacts and details can often be really shocking. Doing the research for *Priapus Agonistes*, I found that the Minotaur's full story was a very loaded historical detail. I read about the Minotaur when I was a kid. I was really into Greek mythology, but of course they don't tell you about the actual conception of the Minotaur and how that all happened. [laughter] So as an adult to come back and read that part of it—you realize why, perhaps with good reason, it was left out of the children's version of mythology. The whole story of the Minotaur's conception is just one example of ancient beliefs that entwine fate, sexuality and family in wild ways. With some aspects of Roman or Greek culture, you feel the continuity of human nature, and then you read something else and realize, nope, we're not the same people! Different conventions, absolutely different ways of structuring the world, different ways of deciding what's right or wrong. History can be very strange and exciting in that way.

CRS

In your process, when do the imaginative flights start to occur?

MRK

Well, the research part of my work and the more creative part of it have an antagonistic relationship. I'll sit down and think, okay, here's forty pages about the Battle of Jutland, for example, and I need to read it because I need to understand what it is, because it's part of what I'm trying to learn or figure out... and I'll be five pages into it, and I'll read a sentence, and another part of my brain will start kicking in and acting out and fighting back against that task. So I'll read "Britannia rules the waves," and the antagonistic voice will say, "Britannia waives the rules." When I sit down to do some reading or some research, I usually try to have another notebook open to catch that antagonistic spillover.

PK

I think of it as being open, rather than antagonistic...an openness to language.

You're reading the given text, which is telling a story and relaying information from history. So what happens is that your openness to the trickiness of language, even if it's supposed to be relaying a historical past, allows punning and wordplay to well up in a situation where it's not "supposed" to, but because it belongs in the context of history you can store that information and then turn it into something else. I've heard you describe it as a sort of welling up of something that you just can't resist.

MRK

You can always sit down and try to make yourself read something for the sake of information, but it's much harder to get yourself to sit down and play, and so often I feel like the playing voice has to be enticed by the opportunity to be disruptive.

CRS

So you have to possess structure to allow "play" to happen, the structure of the text, or the structure of the historical moment that you're exploring...and then you need to rub up against the grain of it, play around with it, twist it. I think the same is true in terms of how you relate to language. You need something to subvert.

MRK

Right, because history can be fascinating, and it can also be boring. It can definitely have the air of "something you *should* be interested in," and you should, if you're a good citizen or a good student, acquire this information. On one hand, you need those conventions of knowledge acquisition if you're going to make a historical work that is relevant to that history—you do have to acquire some of that knowledge—but in the video work I try to give in to the desire to play with it too, or subvert it. That feeling of giving in to play—it's the same as kicking your heels on the chair during school...it's that little voice that makes fun of it all.

CRS

There's a shift in your latest film, *Priapus Agonistes,* in terms of the historic moving into the mythic. You're also playing with the notion of time differently—mixing historical eras with your own history.

MRK

Spending time in Rome really affected how I thought about time. In the earlier

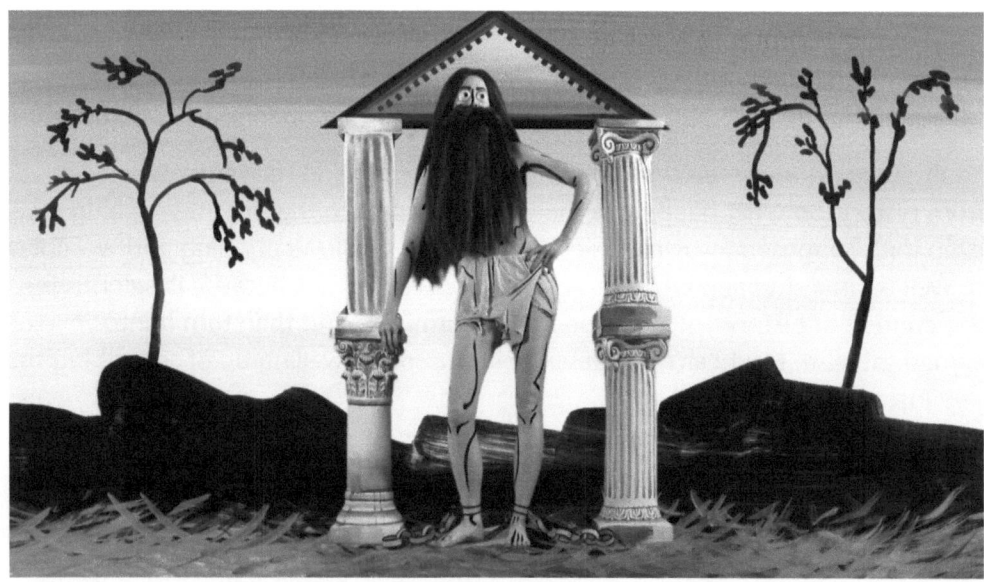

The Syphilis of Sisyphus,
2011
Video still

films, the narrative goes to another time and stays there, drawing on all the details and costumes and voices of that past, in order to evoke the ideas of that time.

The thing that makes Rome totally unique is not how deep the past is, but how cheek-to-jowl all of those eras are. They're in the fabric of the city itself. It's the Coliseum as an ancient Roman amphitheater, and how it then served as a quarry, and how a lot of that travertine marble went into building St. Peter's, something like 1,400 cartloads. The city cannibalizes its own past and uses it. It's a form of appropriation. Romans have always played fast and loose with their own history, and definitely not in a hushed-tone, library-voice kind of way.

CRS
Did being in Rome and experiencing that cheek-to-jowl history firsthand further your fine disregard of the conventional readings of time and place?

MRK
I think it really made me want to do something that was more an aggregate of time. I felt like I was being too safe by staying in a time that wasn't my own, so I started exploring ways to open up the scope of time in our next film. I also really fell in love with Minoan civilization and the Minoan way of painting things, like their pottery and frescoes. It's quite different from the Greeks or the Egyptians: the swirls and checkerboards, the extremities of scale, a small vase with this huge octopus on it, for example. Attic vases, the red-and-black-figure Greek vases, they're amazing and dynamic as well, but everything is so much more pro-portionate. Whereas the Minoans dispense with that whenever they want. Even

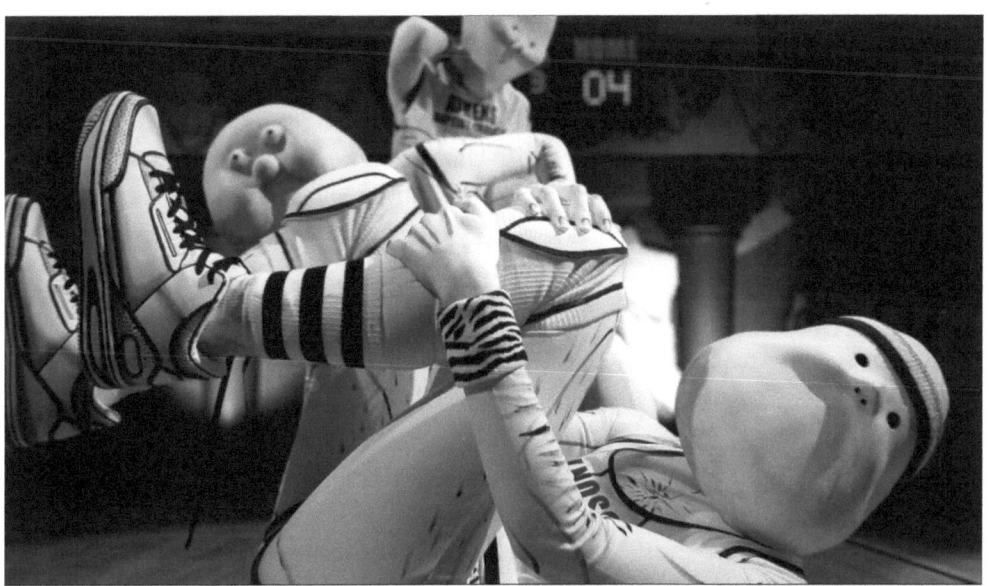

Priapus Agonistes,
2013
Video still

their historians can't help calling the pottery vulgar. I felt like, Minoans are my people! It's like they were the R. Crumb of the ancient world. [laughter]

CRS

I don't think I've ever heard that analogy, but it's a good one!

MRK

It was just one of those moments when I wasn't looking for something and then it all came together. It was a wonderful gift.

CRS

This goes back to the idea you were talking about earlier, about being open to receiving all kinds of information.

PK

That's just what I was thinking. When you look at the Minoan pottery, you see the quickness of it in marks that weren't planned or etched out beforehand. Crooked lines and brushstrokes everywhere—all this stuff! To see that from our point of view now, and to declare an affinity to it with R. Crumb, is something we have the privilege of doing. Whereas in their time, we don't know what kind of cognitive framework they had for why they were working in that way. I feel like the ability for us to do that encapsulates the approach Mary often takes. It's taking the liberty of being a contemporary person and saying, "Oh, that looks like R. Crumb, that style." It can trigger all kinds of ideas for language and humor and anachronisms and things like that.

So when you made the point that *Priapus* actually has this literal time shift depicted in it, for me that's a natural development from something that was already happening, say, in *Sisyphus,* which was set in a specific time period, but we were still using contemporary jokes or humor throughout the piece. There was an anachronistic element, but it was centered in the language, whereas later with *Priapus* the narrative itself is a time mash-up. In addition to the language and contemporary wordplay, there's also the '90s church volleyball team in the labyrinth of the Minotaur. To me it feels like quite a development.

MRK

I think working with mythological characters is another way to navigate the avenues between the individual and the collective. *Priapus* is drawn from a memory I have of watching my dad play volleyball for his church league. On Saturdays I'd tag along and watch his team play. I remember watching, not only my dad, but also the other men of the church, whom we saw every Sunday and also every Wednesday—because in the South you go to church during the week too—and seeing them transform from civic pillars of the community to sweaty red-faced men in short-shorts. You're watching them and they're completely ignoring you. They're completely oblivious to their children and to their roles as fathers. They're just trying to win the darn volleyball game! I remember thinking, who are these people? It was like they were engaging in a form of ancient combat that just stripped them of all their individual qualities, like coming face to face with a kind of primal masculinity. Of course, I think I was just sort of awestruck as a kid, but later I realized there's this whole other thing going on…it was a kid's glimpse into what being an adult really means, and it was scary! So I guess that's what generated the idea of an individual turning into an archetype, or turning into a figure of mythology…watching my father turn into Achilles [laughs]. Understanding that the individual is capable of making those shifts back and forth between individual and archetype was an early lesson my dad gave to me.

CRS
I like the idea that the Minoan "hand" opened up all these avenues to you. What's so striking about your videos is that your own hand is so evident in the films. It adds another layer to the work, a connection to thought, and making, and touch.

MRK
I'm always a little stunned when people talk about the hand-made quality of the work, because it's not an aesthetic that we're choosing among the vast range of available ways of solving problems. I think our films look the way they do because they're essentially two-person shows. We agonize over certain parts. I agonize over the scripts, for example…but when it comes to actually making the work and getting the painting done, then it's a little more…I wouldn't say perfunctory, but we just do it. We make the prop, we design it, and we execute it.

That's the most fun part.

CRS
I find it interesting that you say that's where the fun is. So many artists struggle in the physical making of their work.

PK
Some of that is just the nature of video…having a light hand with the physical objects that we're making, but laboring over the time-based elements. Also, in terms of the perfunctory part of it, there's a pleasure in taking all of the handmade textures and things that Mary gives me to model and then using technological tools to make the images.

CRS
And to make it look so perfunctory.

PK

That's the fun part, the subverting. I've always loved that about making things with "high-end" tools—taking high technology and making it look handmade. And then there's playing with the scale, and all kinds of weird trickery. Like Mary said, "It's fun, it's playful." It can be very spontaneous, because you can change things quickly.

MRK

If you watch films from the first couple of decades of filmmaking, a lot of those movies were made by only six people, maybe a dozen. In *Nosferatu*, they made the whole thing with one camera, which limited the shots they could do. We only have one camera. I think a lot of our work has a resonance with earlier cinema just because the scale is comparable. Pat does cinematography and post-production, I write, act, and direct, and between the two of us we're playing about eight or a dozen people. There's only so far on the scale we can stretch, and when you stretch as far as you can to meet it, then you've got some of the hallmarks, I think, of what can be interpreted as a handmade quality.

CRS

Handmade is the wrong word. I see that now.

MRK

I think Pat was saying that when we make things with digital tools, we try not to make it look too computer-y. But that's literally the one concession we make to a rough-hewn look. In every other part, we're just trying to fulfill the idea. I never think to myself that we have to make it look handmade. We have to make it as good as possible, that's the only benchmark that we're going for with the work. With digital tools, you're constantly encouraged to use right angles and straight planes, so usually we compromise by trying to knock those angles a little off-center and a little out of whack, but that's just to make it look like it's not taking place inside of a video game or something. In every other aspect, we're trying to make it as intense as possible and as close to our ideal as possible.

Diderot's Globe, 2011
Cardboard, metal, and
acrylic paint

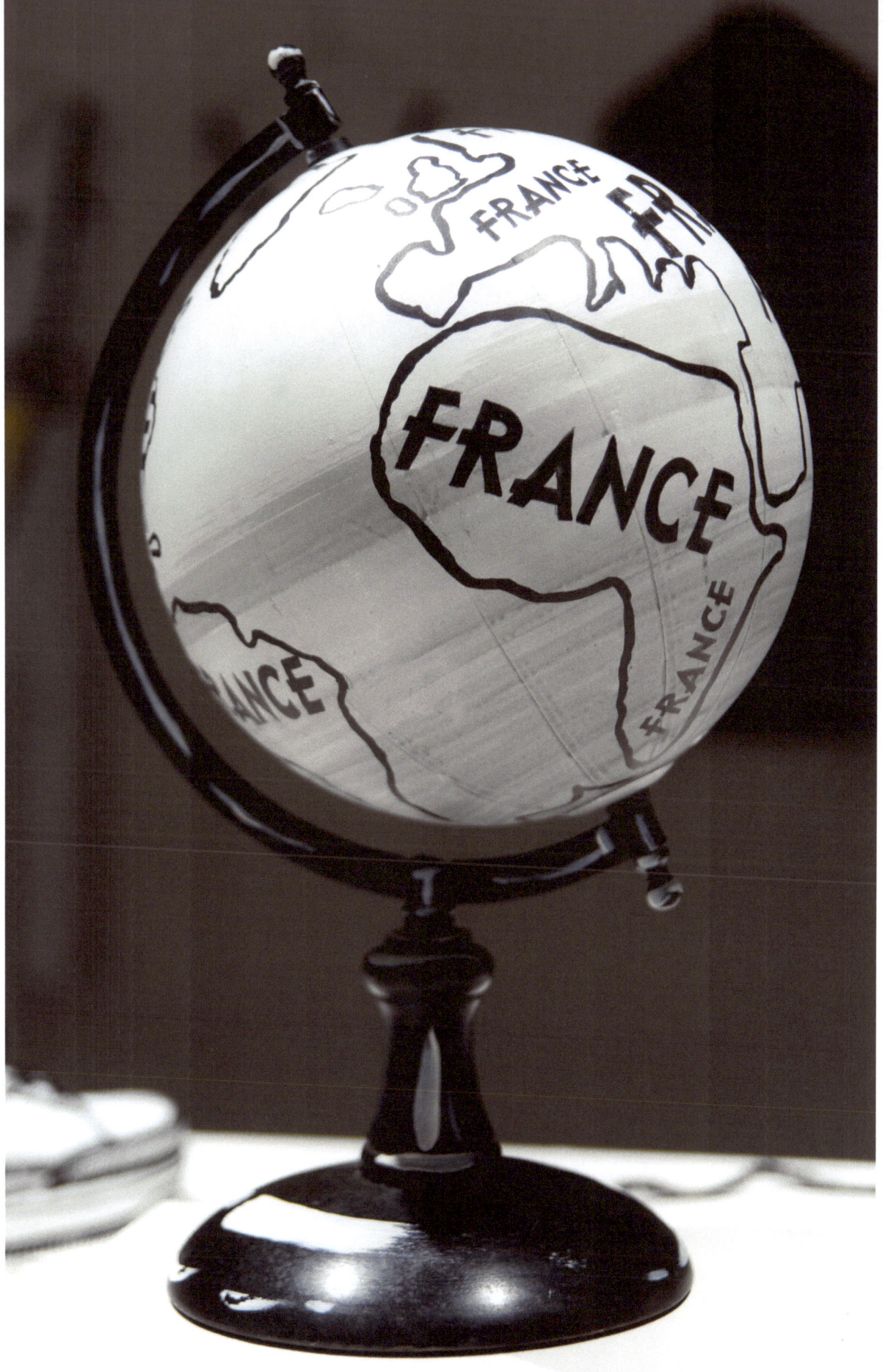

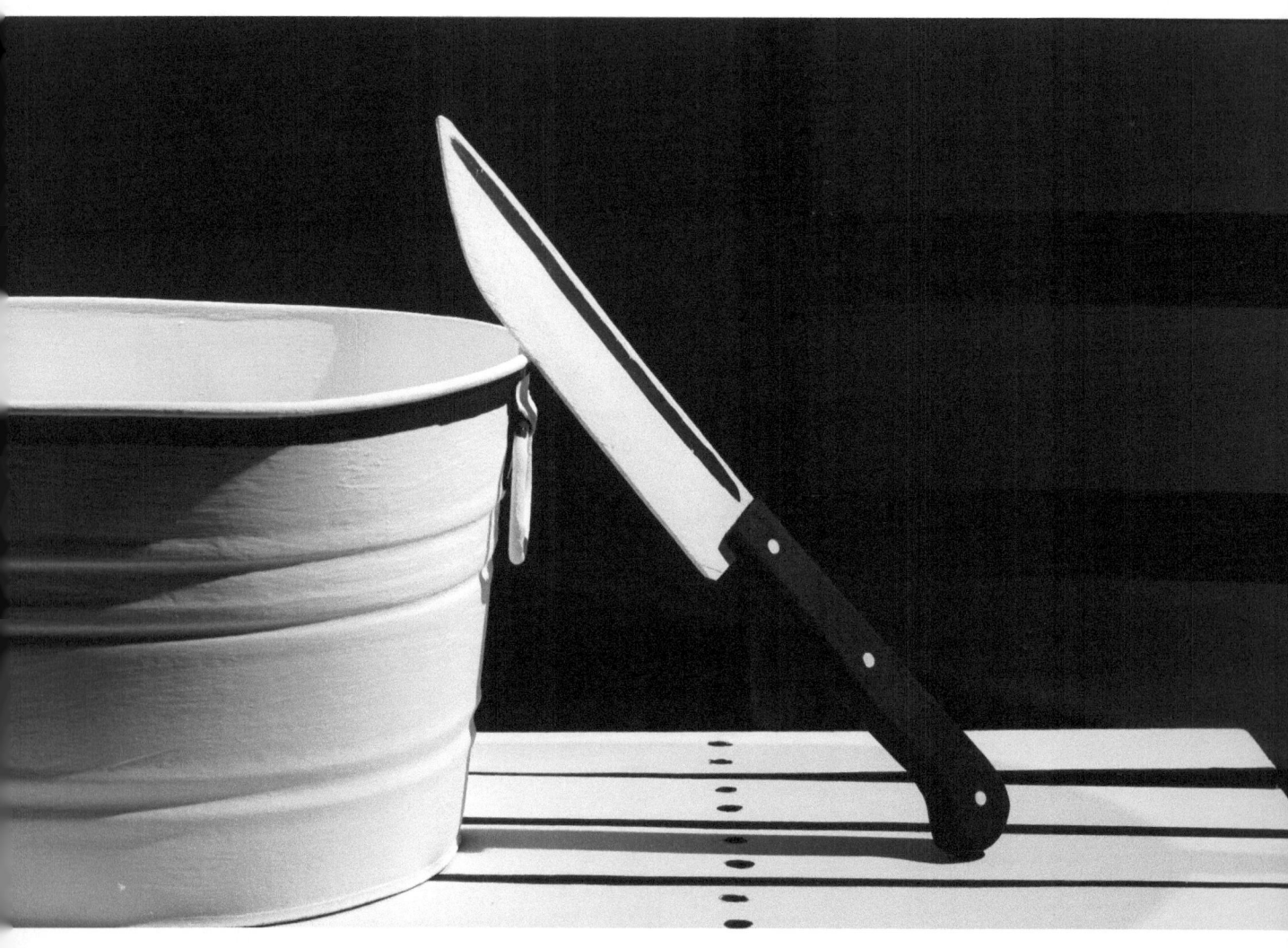

Marat's Bath (detail),
2011
Mixed media

EXHIBITION CHECKLIST

All works by and courtesy of Mary Reid
   Kelley unless otherwise indicated

Videos

Mary Reid Kelley with Patrick Kelley
You Make Me Iliad, 2010
HD video, 14:49 minutes; sound
Courtesy of the artist and Fredericks
   & Freiser Gallery, New York, Susanne
   Vielmetter Los Angeles Projects, and
   Pilar Corrias Gallery, London

Mary Reid Kelley with Patrick Kelley
The Syphilis of Sisyphus, 2011
HD video, 11:02 minutes; sound
Courtesy of the artist and Fredericks
   & Freiser Gallery, New York, Susanne
   Vielmetter Los Angeles Projects, and
   Pilar Corrias Gallery, London

Mary Reid Kelley with Patrick Kelley
Priapus Agonistes, 2013
HD video, 15:09 minutes; sound
Courtesy of the artist and Fredericks
   & Freiser Gallery, New York, Susanne
   Vielmetter Los Angeles Projects, and
   Pilar Corrias Gallery, London

Mary Reid Kelley with Patrick Kelley
Untitled (Set Compositing Demo), 2013
HD video, length variable

Character Drawings and Collages

Medical Officer, 2010
Ink, acrylic paint, and charcoal on paper
12 ⅞ x 9 ¾ inches
Hort Family Collection, New York

Prostitute, 2010
Ink, acrylic paint, and charcoal on paper
11 ½ x 8 ½ inches
Hort Family Collection, New York

Soldier, 2010
Ink, acrylic paint, and charcoal on paper
12 ⅜ x 9 ½ inches
Hort Family Collection, New York

Soldier in Helmet 1, 2010
Ink, acrylic paint, and charcoal on paper
21 ¾ x 29 ⅜ inches
Hort Family Collection, New York

Chiffonniers' Vins, 2011
Collage and watercolor on paper
11 ⅝ x 8 ¼ inches
Courtesy of Fredericks & Freiser Gallery,
   New York

Dandy Saltimbanque, 2011
Collage, watercolor, and acrylic paint on
   paper
20 ½ x 12 inches
Collection of Leslie Cecil and Creighton
   Michael

Fort! Fort!, 2011
Collage, watercolor, and acrylic paint on
   paper
9 ½ x 13 ⅞ inches
Courtesy of Fredericks & Freiser Gallery,
   New York

Haussmann's Slum, 2011
Collage, acrylic paint, ink, and charcoal
   on paper
11 x 14 inches
Anonymous

Ideal Vins, 2011
Ink and charcoal on paper
11 x 8 ½ inches
Courtesy of Fredericks & Freiser Gallery,
New York

Marie Antoinette's Bed, 2011
Collage and acrylic paint on paper
11 x 14 inches
Collection of Robert Hobbs and Jean
Crutchfield

Mogadora, 2011
Collage, watercolor, and acrylic paint on
paper
16 ³/₈ x 9 ½ inches
Courtesy of Fredericks & Freiser Gallery,
New York

Robespierre, 2011
Collage, acrylic paint, ink, and charcoal
on paper
11 x 14 inches
Collection of Jennifer Danner

Sisyphus (Chiffonniers' Vins), 2011
Collage and watercolor on paper
20 x 16 inches
Collection of Robert Hobbs and Jean
Crutchfield

Working Objects for *You Make Me Iliad*

Basin, 2010
Metal and acrylic paint
8 ⁵/₈ x 17 ¾ inches

Douchebag, 2010
Rubber, plastic, and acrylic paint
12 x 7 x 1 ¼ inches

"Gott Mit Uns" Mittens, 2010
Wool and yarn
Three objects: 10 ½ x 4 inches each

Medical Officer's Eyes, 2010
Polymer clay and acrylic paint
2 ¹/₈ x 1 ⁵/₈ x 1 inches

Medical Officer's Mercury Chloride
Bottle, 2010
Glass, paper, and ink
8 ½ x 3 ¼ x 1 ¾ inches

Medical Officer's Pickelhaube, 2010
Plastic, polymer clay, Styrofoam, and
acrylic paint
8 x 9 ½ x 7 ¾ inches

Soldier's Helmet, 2010
Plastic, buttons, polymer clay, and
acrylic paint
6 x 11 ¼ x 9 ¼ inches

Soldier's Uniform, 2010
Wool, polymer clay, and acrylic paint;
"Gott Mit Uns" buckle and belt: foam,
cardboard, and acrylic paint
46 x 19 inches

Bismarck, 2010
8 ½ x 5 ½ inches
Corset Girls, 2010
9 ¾ x 6 ¾ inches
Goethe, 2010
8 ⁵/₈ x 6 ¾ inches
Hat Girl, 2010
10 ¾ x 5 ¾ inches
Homer, 2010
6 ³/₈ x 4 ⁵/₈ inches
Kaiser, 2010
8 ½ x 7 ⁵/₈ inches
Kant, 2010
6 ¾ x 5 ¾ inches
Leibniz, 2010
8 ¹/₈ x 6 ¾ inches
Lessing, 2010
8 x 5 ¾ inches
Nietzsche, 2010
6 ¹/₈ x 6 inches
Shakespeare, 2010
6 ¾ x 5 ⁵/₈ inches
Ski Girl, 2010
8 ¹/₈ x 6 ¼ inches
Wagner, 2010
4 ⁷/₈ x 4 ¼ inches
Ink and graphite on vellum
Hort Family Collection, New York

**Working Objects for *The Syphilis of
Sisyphus* (2011)**

Charlotte Corday's Gown, 2011
Cloth
55 x 29 inches
Courtesy of Fredericks & Freiser Gallery,
New York

Dandy's Coat 1, 2011
Cloth, felt, polymer clay, and acrylic
paint
31 x 25 inches
Courtesy of Fredericks & Freiser Gallery,
New York

Dandy's Coat 2, 2011
Cloth, felt, polymer clay, and acrylic
paint
39 ¼ x 25 inches
Courtesy of Fredericks & Freiser Gallery,
New York

Dandy's Coat 3, 2011
Cloth, ribbon, felt, polymer clay, and
acrylic paint; Vest: linen, ribbon, and
acrylic paint
37 x 24 inches
Courtesy of Fredericks & Freiser Gallery,
New York

Dandy's Top Hat, 2011
Felt, plastic, ribbon, and oil stick
7 ⁷/₈ x 11 x 9 inches

Diderot's Globe, 2011
Cardboard, metal, and acrylic paint
14 ½ x 9 x 8 inches

Flowers, 2011
Plastic and acrylic paint
Two objects: 27 x 6 and 24 x 5 ½ inches
each

Listening Tube, 2011
Cardboard, tape, and acrylic paint
11 x 2 ¼ inches

Marat's Bath, 2011
Platform: wood and acrylic paint,
53 ⁷/₈ x 17 ¾ x 1 ½ inches
Chairs (two): wood, canvas, and acrylic
paint, 43 ¹/₈ x 19 ⁷/₈ x 16 inches each
Tub: metal and acrylic paint,
8 ¾ x 24 ⁵/₈ x 14 inches
Knife: wood and acrylic paint,
16 x 1 ¾ x ¾ inches

Milk Bottle, 2011
Plastic and acrylic paint
9 x 3 ¼ inches

Morel, 2011
Polymer clay and acrylic paint
6 ¹/₈ x 1 ⁵/₈ inches

Morel Hat, 2011
Insulating foam sealant, wire, papier-
mâché, and acrylic paint
19 ³/₈ x 12 x 11 inches

Mushroom Background, 2011
Acrylic paint on paper
9 ½ x 13 inches

Mushroom Hat, 2011
Styrofoam, papier-mâché, and acrylic
  paint
8 ½ x 12 inches

Nature Background, 2011
Acrylic paint on paper
9 ³/₈ x 13 inches

Pear, 2011
Plastic and acrylic paint
4 x 3 ½ inches

Saltimbanques' Costumes, 2011
Cotton, Styrofoam, thread, ribbon, and
  acrylic paint
Four costumes: 52 ½ x 23 inches each

Samson's Chains, 2011
Paper, glue, and acrylic paint
Two objects: 14 x 2 ½ x 2 ½ inches each

Samson's Column Fragments, 2011
Plaster and acrylic paint
Dimensions variable

Sisyphus's Apple, 2011
Plastic, polymer clay, and acrylic paint
4 ½ x 3 inches

Sisyphus's Bouquet, 2011
Plastic and acrylic paint
13 x 14 inches

Sisyphus's Eyes, 2011
Polymer clay and acrylic paint
1 ½ x 1 ³/₈ x ¾ inches

Sisyphus's Gown, 2011
Cloth, ribbon, tassel, lace, foam, and
  hoop skirt; Necklace: polymer clay
  and acrylic paint
53 x 45 inches
Courtesy of Fredericks & Freiser Gallery,
  New York

Sisyphus's Hand Mirror, 2011
Plastic, glass, and acrylic paint
10 x 5 ⁷/₈ x ½ inches

Sisyphus's Shoes, 2011
Leather, tape, cardboard, and
  acrylic paint
4 ½ x 11 ½ x 3 ⁷/₈ inches each
Courtesy of Fredericks & Freiser Gallery,
  New York

Sisyphus's Straitjacket, 2011
Cotton, thread, ribbon, and acrylic paint
26 ½ x 19 inches

Sisyphus's Table, 2011
Table: wood and acrylic paint,
  22 ½ x 19 ¾ inches
Wine Bottle: glass and acrylic paint,
  13 ⁵/₈ x 4 ¹/₈ inches
Baguette: foam and spray paint,
  22 ½ x 3 inches

Sisyphus's Vanity, 2011
Vanity: wood, mirror, metal, and acrylic
  paint, 50 ¼ x 28 x 16 inches
Stool: wood, upholstery, and acrylic
  paint, 17 x 18 x 15 inches
Lime: plastic and acrylic paint,
  1 ³/₈ x 3 ½ x 1 ¾ inches
Lace: black lace, 5 ½ inches diameter
Brush: wood, bristles, and acrylic paint,
  1 ¾ x 5 ¼ x 3 ¹/₈ inches
Chalice: plastic and acrylic paint,
  7 ³/₈ x 3 ½ inches
Paint Brush (large): plastic and acrylic
  paint, 9 ¾ x ½ inches
Paint Brush (small): plastic and acrylic
  paint, 7 ¾ x ³/₈ inches
Makeup Pot and Feather: ceramic,
  feather, and acrylic paint,
  5 ½ x 2 ¼ inches
Mortar and Pestle: stoneware and
  acrylic paint, 3 ½ x 5 ¾ x 4 ½ inches
Wine Bottle: glass and acrylic paint,
  12 ¼ x 3 ¼ inches
Flowers (two): plastic and acrylic paint,
  27 x 6 and 24 x 5 ½ inches
Banana: plastic and acrylic paint,
  7 x 1 ½ x 2 ½ inches
Makeup Pot (white): ceramic and acrylic
  paint, 1 x 3 inches
Bottle (oval): glass and acrylic paint,
  4 x 2 x ⁷/₈ inches

Sisyphus's Wig, n.d.
Synthetic hair
10 ½ x 10 ½ inches
Courtesy of Fredericks & Freiser Gallery,
  New York

Small Makeup Pot (black), 2011
Ceramic and acrylic paint
1 x 3 inches

Small Bottle (square), 2011
Glass and acrylic paint
5 ¹/₈ x 1 ⁵/₈ x 1 ⁵/₈ inches

Stethoscope, 2011
Plastic and rubber
23 ½ x 9 ¼ x 2 ⁵/₈ inches

Texture (Cobblestones), 2011
Oil and acrylic paint on Stonehenge
  paper, two sheets
29 ⁵/₈ x 44 ¼ inches

Texture (Marble), 2011
Acrylic paint on paper
8 ¼ x 10 inches

Texture (Stripe 1), 2011
Acrylic paint on paper
10 x 11 ¼ inches

Texture (Stripe 2), 2011
Acrylic paint on paper
8 ¾ x 13 ⁷/₈ inches

Texture (Wallpaper), 2011
Acrylic paint on paper
11 ¼ x 9 ⁵/₈ inches

Texture (Wood 1), 2011
Oil stick on paper
7 ⁷/₈ x 10 inches

Texture (Wood 2), 2011
Oil stick on paper
8 ¼ x 11 inches

Wine Bottle, 2011
Glass and acrylic paint
11 ½ x 2 ¾ inches

Wine Bottles, 2011
Glass and acrylic paint
Three objects: 11 ¾ x 3 inches each

Wine Glasses, 2011
Glass and acrylic paint
Two objects: 6 x 1 ⁷/₈ inches each

**Working Objects for *Priapus Agonistes*
(2013)**

Ariadne's Costume, 2013
Fabric, ribbon, and acrylic paint;
    Necklace: polymer clay, and acrylic
    paint
55 x 24 x 10 inches

Ariadne's Mask, 2013
Neoprene, gesso, polymer clay, and
    acrylic paint; Wig: synthetic hair and
    tape
20 x 10 x 5 inches

Ariadne's Spindle, 2013
Wood, polymer clay, acrylic paint, yarn,
    and thread
12 ½ x 2 ⅛ inches

Baby Minotaur, 2013
Plastic, polymer clay, and acrylic paint
13 x 6 ½ x 5 ½ inches

Bananas
Plastic and acrylic paint
Three objects: 7 x 1 ½ x 2 ½ inches each

Chicken Feet, 2013
Rubber and acrylic paint
Two objects: 7 ¾ x 1 ⅝ x ⅞ inches each

Daedalus's Hammer, 2013
Metal, wood, and acrylic paint
12 ½ x 4 ½ x 1 inches

Daedalus's Mask, 2013
Neoprene, gesso, polymer clay, and
    acrylic paint; Wig: synthetic hair;
    Visor: foam
11 ½ x 9 ½ x 7 ¾ inches

Hades's Mask, 2013
Rubber and acrylic paint
1 ⅜ x 2 ½ x 2 ⅜ inches

Labyrinth Graffiti (Abomination), 2013
Ink on paper
7 ⅜ x 10 ⅞ inches

Labyrinth Graffiti (Ariadne), 2013
Ink on paper
10 ⅞ x 8 ⅜ inches

Labyrinth Graffiti (Come Redeemer),
    2013
Ink on paper
7 ½ x 10 ⅞ inches

Labyrinth Graffiti (Hall-Shitter), 2013
Ink on paper
7 ⅜ x 11 inches

Labyrinth Graffiti (Hand), 2013
Acrylic paint on paper
10 ¾ x 8 ⅜ inches

Labyrinth Graffiti (Help), 2013
Acrylic paint on paper
10 ⅞ x 8 ⅜ inches

Labyrinth Graffiti (Malcontent), 2013
Ink on paper
7 ½ x 11 inches

Labyrinth Graffiti (Mooooo), 2013
Ink on paper
11 x 8 ½ inches

Labyrinth Graffiti (Murderer), 2013
Ink on paper
7 ⅜ x 10 ⅞ inches

Labyrinth Graffiti (Pasiphae), 2013
Ink on paper
10 ⅞ x 8 ½ inches

Labyrinth Graffiti (Priapus Agonistes),
    2013
Ink on paper
6 ¼ x 11 inches

Labyrinth Graffiti (This Way), 2013
Ink on paper
7 ½ x 11 inches

Labyrinth Graffiti (Your End), 2013
Ink on paper
7 ¼ x 11 inches

Midwife's Mask, 2013
Neoprene, gesso, polymer clay, and
    acrylic paint; Wig: synthetic hair;
    Snood: cotton and ribbon
9 x 6 ⅜ x 4 ¾ inches

Minoan Frescoes, 2013
Ink, oil stick, and acrylic paint on paper
Dimensions variable

Minotaur's Costume, 2013
Garment: fabric, acrylic paint, and yarn;
    Mask: neoprene, gesso, polymer clay,
    Stonehenge paper, rubber, felt, and
    acrylic paint; Watch: elastic band,
    polymer clay, and acrylic paint
66 x 18 x 14 inches

Minotaur Victim's Skeleton, 2013
Plastic and acrylic paint
Dimensions variable

Minotaur Victim's Skeleton Hand with
    Watch, 2013
Plastic, elastic band, polymer clay, and
    acrylic paint
14 ¾ x 4 ½ x 1 ⅝ inches

Minotaur Victim's Skull, 2013
Foam and acrylic paint
5 ⅝ x 5 ½ x 6 ½ inches

Minotaur Victim's Sneakers (Hightop),
    2013
Sneakers and acrylic paint
5 ⅝ x 11 ½ x 4 ⅛ inches each

Minotaur Victim's Sneakers (Velcro),
    2013
Sneakers and acrylic paint
5 ¼ x 12 ⅜ x 4 ½ inches each

Minotaur Victim's Watch, 2013
Elastic band, polymer clay, and acrylic
    paint
2 ¼ x 1 ¼ x 1 ⅜ inches

Miss Barley's Mask, 2013
Neoprene, gesso, headband, polymer
    clay, and acrylic paint; Wig: synthetic
    hair
26 ¾ x 9 x 5 ¼ inches

Miss Millet's Mask, 2013
Neoprene, gesso, headband, polymer
    clay, and acrylic paint; Wig: synthetic
    hair
36 x 10 ½ x 5 ¼ inches

Miss Spelt's Costume, 2013
Fabric, ribbon, decal, and acrylic paint
56 x 25 inches

Miss Spelt's Mask, 2013
Neoprene, gesso, polymer clay, and
  acrylic paint; Wig: synthetic hair
22 x 11 x 5 inches

Pasiphae's Shoes, 2013
Leather and acrylic paint
6 ¼ x 10 ⅝ x 3 ½ inches each

Pasiphae's Sunglasses, 2013
Plastic and acrylic paint
5 ¾ x 2 x 6 inches

Pasiphae's Swimsuit, 2013
Lycra, yarn, and acrylic paint
26 ½ x 13 ½ inches

Pasiphae's Tissue Box, 2013
Cardboard, tissues, and acrylic paint
2 ¼ x 9 x 4 ¾ inches

Pasiphae's Towel, n.d.
Cotton
Folded: 3 x 14 ½ x 14 ½ inches

Pasiphae's Wig, 2013
Synthetic hair and tape
17 x 9 ½ inches

Persephone's Mask, 2013
Rubber and acrylic paint
1 ⅜ x 2 ½ x 2 ⅜ inches

Priapus's Banana, 2013
Plastic and acrylic paint
7 x 1 ½ x 2 ½ inches

Priapus's Costume, 2013
Spandex, suspenders, cotton, plastic,
  decal, and acrylic paint
52 x 11 ½ inches

Priapus's Fish, 2013
Polymer clay and acrylic paint
6 ⅛ x 2 ¼ x ½ inches

Priapus's Peppers, 2013
Plastic and acrylic paint
Two objects: 6 ¾ x 1 ½ x 1 ⅛ inches
  each

Priapus's Rooster Head, 2013
Rubber, polymer clay, and acrylic paint
7 x 4 ½ x 1 ½ inches

Puppet "Dick", 2013
Felt, ribbon, and wood
6 ½ x 3 inches

Puppet "Hairy", 2013
Felt, ribbon, and wood
6 ¼ x 5 ⅜ inches

Referee's Shirt, 2013
Polyester
31 ½ x 25 ½ inches

Venus's Bracelet (Large), 2013
Plastic, polymer clay, and acrylic paint
1 ⅜ x 3 ½ inches

Venus's Bracelet (Small), 2013
Plastic and acrylic paint
½ x 3 ½ x 2 ⅞ inches

Venus's Bustier, 2013
Cloth, ribbon, and acrylic paint
23 ¼ x 12 inches

Venus's Lotion, 2013
Plastic and acrylic paint
5 ¾ x 1 ¾ x 1 inches

Venus's Mask, 2013
Neoprene, gesso, polymer clay, and
  acrylic paint; Wig: synthetic hair
13 ¾ x 15 ½ x 6 inches

Venus's Necklace, 2013
Polymer clay and acrylic paint
10 x 7 inches

Venus's Rings, 2013
Metal, polymer clay, and acrylic paint
Four objects: largest 1 ½ inches
  diameter

Volleyball (Ba'al), 2013
Volleyball and acrylic paint
7 ½ inches diameter

Volleyball Clipboard, 2013
Particleboard, metal, paper, inkjet print,
  tape, acrylic paint, and marker
9 x 12 ½ x 1 ⅝ inches

Volleyball Player (Nude), 2013
Lycra, foam, and acrylic paint
51 ½ x 23 inches

Volleyball Player's Mask, 2013
Neoprene, gesso, polymer clay, and
  acrylic paint; Wig: synthetic hair
13 x 12 x 5 ½ inches

Volleyball Player's Socks, 2013
Cotton and acrylic paint
Two objects: 14 x 3 ¼ inches each

Volleyball Player's Uniform (Athens Tank
  Top), 2013
Cotton, decal, and acrylic paint
29 x 10 inches

Volleyball Player 's Uniform (Athens Tee
  Shirt), 2013
Cotton, ribbon, decal, and acrylic paint
30 ½ x 16 ½ inches

Volleyball Player's Uniform (Knossos
  Tank Top), 2013
Cotton, ribbon, decal, and acrylic paint
25 x 14 inches

Volleyball Player's Uniform (Knossos Tee
  Shirt), 2013
Cotton, ribbon, decal, and acrylic paint
28 ¼ x 23 inches

Volleyball Player's Uniform
  (Polo Shirt), 2013
Cotton, acrylic paint, and ribbon
31 ½ x 23 inches

BIOGRAPHY

Born in Greenville, South Carolina in 1979
Lives and works in Olivebridge, New York

Education
2009   M.F.A. Yale University, New Haven, Connecticut
2001   B.A. St. Olaf College, Northfield, Minnesota

Solo Exhibitions
2013   *Sadie, The Saddest Sadist* and *Priapus Agonistes*, Yale University Art Gallery, New Haven, Connecticut

Mary Reid Kelley, Institute of Contemporary Art, Boston

The Syphilis of Sisyphus, The Contemporary Austin, Austin, Texas

Priapus Agonistes, Susanne Vielmetter Los Angeles Projects, Los Angeles

2012   *The Syphilis of Sisyphus*, The Box at Wexner Center for the Arts, Columbus, Ohio

H/Qu: Mary Reid Kelley with Patrick Kelley, Bard Center for Curatorial Studies, Annandale-on-Hudson, New York

Performing Histories: Mary Reid Kelley, Salina Art Center, Salina, Kansas

2011   *The Syphilis of Sisyphus*, Fredericks & Freiser Gallery, New York

2010   *You Make Me Iliad*, Pilar Corrias Gallery, London

Sadie, The Saddest Sadist, Susanne Vielmetter Los Angeles Projects, Los Angeles

2009   *Sadie, The Saddest Sadist*, Fredericks & Freiser Gallery, New York

2007   *Bring Superior Forces To Bear*, Rochester Art Center, Rochester, New York

2006   *Paper Union*, Christensen Center Art Gallery, Augsburg College, Minneapolis, Minnesota

Group Exhibitions
2014   *Pale Fire*, LeRoy Neiman Gallery, Columbia University, New York

Rose Video 03: Maria Lassnig and Mary Reid Kelly, Rose Art Museum, Brandeis University, Waltham, Massachusetts

2013   *Through the Eyes of Texas: Masterworks from the Alumni Collections*, Blanton Museum of Art, University of Texas at Austin, Austin, Texas

2012   *Pencil Pushed*, Ewing Gallery of Art & Architecture, University of Tennessee, Knoxville, Tennessee

Re-generation, MACRO Testaccio, Rome

Buy My Bananas, Kate Werble Gallery, New York

Rear View Mirror, Space B Gallery, New York

Weighted Words, Zabludowicz Collection, London

2011   *Words*, Brand 10 Art Space, Fort Worth, Texas

Doublespeak, Utah Museum of Contemporary Art, Salt Lake City, Utah

Stagecraft, Contemporary Art Museum, University of Southern Florida, Tampa, Florida

Images from a Floating World, Fredericks & Freiser Gallery, New York

Texture.txt, Regina Rex, Brooklyn, New York

2010   *Mash-Up: Splicing Life*, UConn Contemporary Art Galleries, University of Connecticut, Storrs, Connecticut

The Dissolve: Eighth International Biennial Exhibition, SITE Santa Fe, Santa Fe, New Mexico

Fast Forward 2: The Power of Motion, ZKM Center for Art and Media, Karlsruhe, Germany

Ludicrous!, Institute of Contemporary Art, Philadelphia

2008   *Will Happiness Find Me?*, Marvelli Gallery, New York

Interval(le)s, Journal, University of Liege Publications

2006   *Uncle Tom to Peeping Tom*, Wisconsin African American Women's Center, Milwaukee, Wisconsin

2005   *Pinko Commies*, Altered Esthetics Gallery, Minneapolis, Minnesota

2004   *Draw,* Soo Visual Arts Center, Minneapolis, Minnesota

BIBLIOGRAPHY

Monographs

Porter, Jenelle. *Mary Reid Kelley*. Boston: Institute of Contemporary Art, 2013.

Exhibition Catalogues

De Wachter, Ellen Mara. *Weighted Words*. London: Zabludowicz Collection, 2012.

Goetz, Ingvild, and Stephan Urbaschek, eds. *Fast Forward 2: The Power of Motion*. Karlsruhe, Germany: ZKM Center for Art and Media, 2010.

Lewis, Sarah, and Daniel Belasco. *The Dissolve: Eighth International Biennial Exhibition*. Santa Fe: SITE Santa Fe, 2010.

Books

Price, Matt, ed. *Vitamin D2: New Perspective in Drawing*. London and New York: Phaidon Press, 2013.

Sollins, Susan, Marybeth Sollins, and Wesley Miller. *Art 21: Art in the Twenty-First Century, Season 6*. New York: Art21 Inc., 2012.

Articles and Reviews

Anonymous. "Goings On About Town: Mary Reid Kelley," *The New Yorker,* January 9, 2012.

Beckman, Ericka. "Mary Reid Kelley, Sadie the Saddest Sadist," *Artforum*, December 2011.

Berkovitch, Ellen. "SITE Santa Fe 8th International Biennial," *artUS*, Issue #29, 2010.

Boucher, Brian. "Mary Reid Kelley, In Plain Frenglish," *Art in America*, November 2009, online.

_____. "Mary Reid Kelley," *Art in America*, November 2009.

Casid, Jill H. "Cis," *Journal of Visual Culture*, August 2012.

Davis, Ben. "Finding the Reason in Mary Reid Kelley's Mad Rhymes About French History," *Artinfo*, January 6, 2012, online.

Forde, Kate. "Mary Reid Kelley," *Frieze,* November–December 2010.

Johnson, Ken. "Mary Reid Kelley: The Syphilis of Sisyphus," *The New York Times,* December 21, 2011, C31.

Kazanjian, Dodie. "The Body Eccentric," *Vogue*, February 2010.

Landi, Ann. "History in the Making," *ARTnews*, January 2011.

_____. "The Dissolve," *ARTnews,* January 2011.

Madoff, Steven Henry. "Mary Reid Kelley," *Artforum*, November 2009.

McClemont, Doug. "Reviews: Mary Reid Kelley," *ARTnews,* March 2012.

McQuaid, Cate. "Images speaking of desire and fear at the ICA," *The Boston Globe*, August 1, 2013.

Mizota, Sharon. "Modern Girl," *Los Angeles Times,* May 21, 2010.

Ollman, Leah. "Everything Moves, All The Time," *Art in America*, October 2010.

Pearse, Emma. "Artist Mary Reid Kelley Goes to War," *New York Magazine,* July 14, 2008, online.

Robecchi, Michele. "Mary Reid Kelley," *Flash Art International*, November–December 2010.

Ryan, Bartholomew. "Marx on My Lenin: Mary Reid Kelley," *Metropolis M,* April 2010.

Smith, Roberta. "Make Room for Video, Performance and Paint," *The New York Times*, December 31, 2009, AR23.

Sorkin, Jenni. "Softer Atrocities: An Introduction to Mary Reid Kelley's *The Syphilis of Sisyphus*," *Gulf Coast Literary Journal*, Fall 2013.

Storr, Robert. "Moving Images," *Frieze*, September 2009.

_____. "So It Goes," *Frieze*, November–December 2009.

Vilas, Amber. "Mary Reid Kelley in New York," *ArtInfo*, September 25, 2009, online.

Interviews

Allen, Emma. "Verbal Play and Venereal Disease: A Q&A with Mary Reid Kelley," *ArtInfo,* June 2010, online.

Green, Tyler. "Modern Art Notes Podcast," July 29, 2013, online.

Sollins, Susan. "Art in the Twenty-First Century" in "History," PBS, season 6, episode 3, April 28, 2012.

Thomson, Allese. "500 Words: Mary Reid Kelley," www.artforum.com, August 14, 2013.

Mary Reid Kelley: Working Objects and Videos

Published on the occasion of the exhibition
Mary Reid Kelley: Working Objects and Videos, curated
by Daniel Belasco, on view from January 22–April 13,
2014 in the Alice and Horace Chandler and
North Galleries at the Samuel Dorsky Museum of Art,
State University of New York at New Paltz; and from
July 10–October 12, 2014 at the University Art Museum,
University at Albany, State University of New York.

Mary Reid Kelley: Working Objects and Videos is
organized by the Samuel Dorsky Museum of Art in
partnership with the University Art Museum,
University at Albany.

Support for the Dorsky Museum's exhibitions and
programs is provided by Friends of the Samuel Dorsky
Museum of Art and the State University of New York at
New Paltz. Funding for the University Art Museum's
exhibitions, publications, and programs is provided by
UAlbany's Office of the President and Office of the
Provost, The University at Albany Foundation, and the
Ellsworth Kelly Foundation.

Mary Reid Kelley and Patrick Kelley would like to
acknowledge the Shifting Foundation and the
American Academy in Rome.

Published by the Samuel Dorsky Museum of Art
State University of New York at New Paltz
One Hawk Drive
New Paltz, New York 12561

Design by Zheng Hu
Edited by Jeanne Finley
Photography by Patrick Kelley
Printed by Lightning Source
Distributed by the State University of New York Press
(www.sunypress.edu)

ISBN: 978-0-615-70149-3

COVER: Marat's Bath, installation view,
Samuel Dorsky Museum of Art
INSIDE COVER: Working Objects, installation view,
Samuel Dorsky Museum of Art
BACK INSIDE COVER: Working Objects, installation view,
Samuel Dorsky Museum of Art

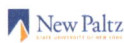 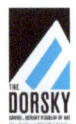 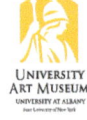

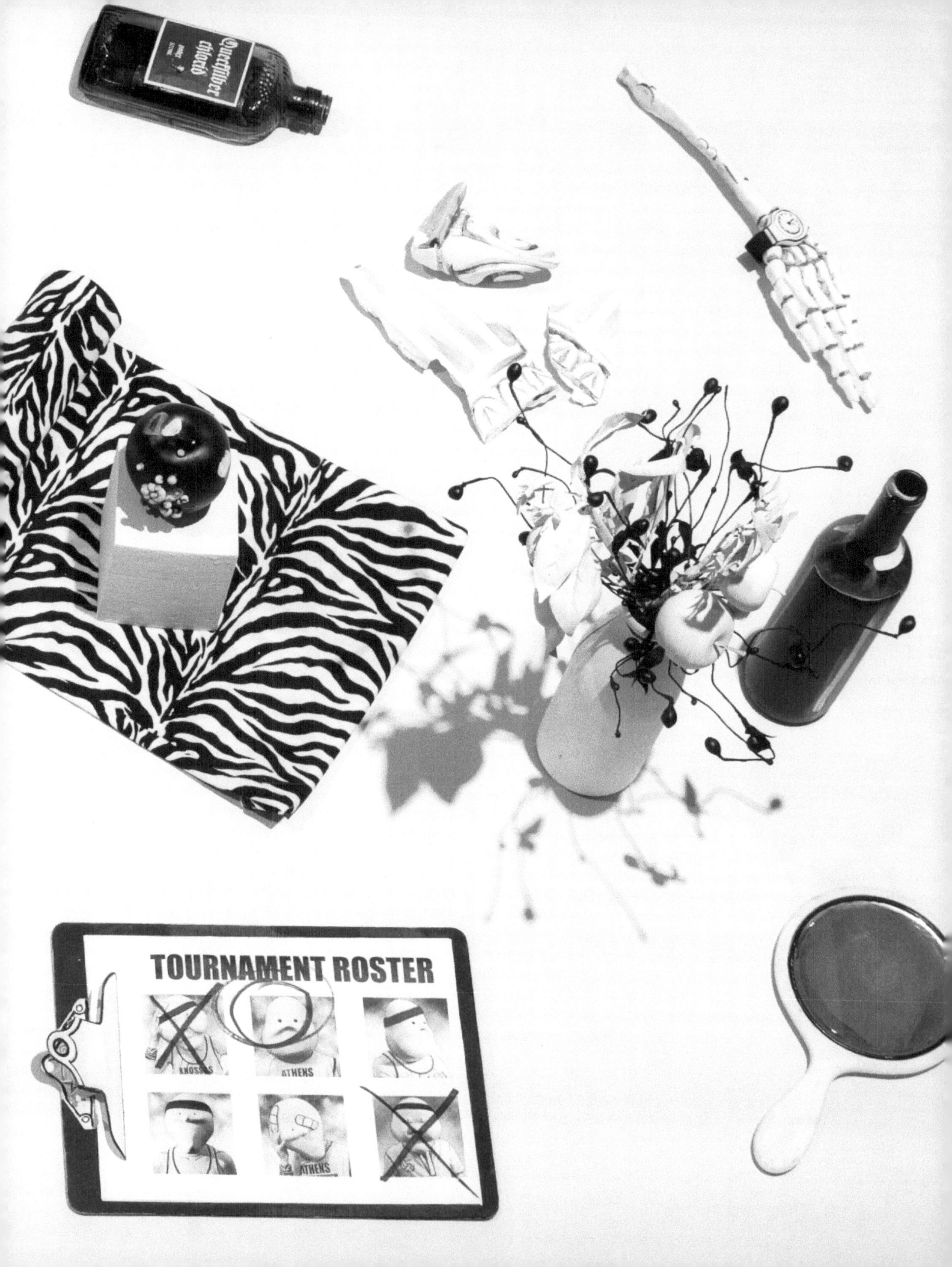

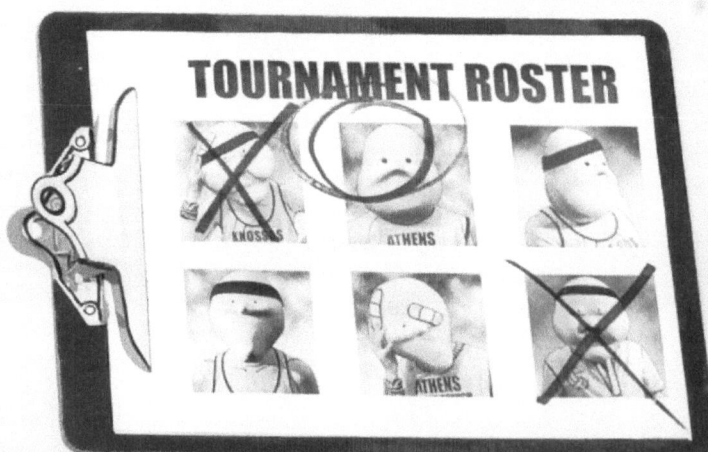

TOURNAMENT ROSTER

KNOSSOS | ATHENS

ATHENS

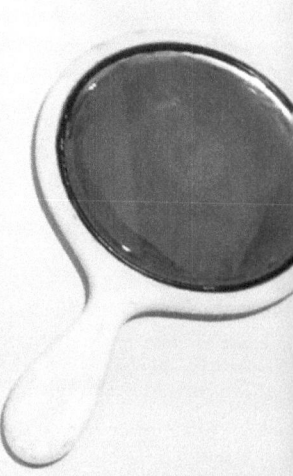

www.ingramcontent.com/pod-product-compliance
Lightning Source LLC
Chambersburg PA
CBHW050855180526
45159CB00007B/2683